36 LETTERS

One Family's Story

For my parents, Sarah and Barney Moss, my brother Marty,
and my children Marnie, Jonathan and Eve, and Nicole.
My past and my future.

36 LETTERS

One Family's Story

JOAN SOHN

The Jewish Publication Society

A Family Legacy Book

2010 - 5771

The Jewish Publication Society
2100 Arch Street, 2nd floor
Philadelphia, PA 19103
www.jewishpub.org

Design by Joan Sohn.
Composition by Janet Tonello, Lakeside Graphics.

Manufactured in the United States of America

11 12   10 9 8 7 6 5 4 3 2

ISBN: 978-0-8276-0926-6
Library of Congress Cataloging-in-Publication Data
Sohn, Joan.
36 letters : one family's story / by Joan Sohn. -- 1st ed.
    p. cm.
 Includes bibliographical references.
 ISBN 978-0-8276-0926-6
 1. Korman family. 2. Korman family--Correspondence. 3. Jews--Be-
larus--Brest--Biography. 4. Jews--Belarus--Brest--Correspondence. 5.
Jews, Belarussian--United States--Correspondence. I. Title. II. Title:
Thirty six letters.
 DS135.B383.C677 2010
 929'.20973--dc22
  2010017050

JPS is a nonprofit educational association and the oldest and foremost

publisher of Judaica in English in North America. The mission of JPS is

to enhance Jewish culture by promoting the dissemination of religious

and secular works, in the United States and abroad, to all individuals

and institutions interested in past and contemporary Jewish life.

CONTENTS

LOST AND FOUND

Mom's Russian embroidery patterns.

We have a family treasure.

Pop, my grandfather Hyman Korman, kept a bag filled with letters. You could not imagine more humble housing for a treasure. These thirty-six letters, some in their original envelopes, filled a small brown Kraft-paper grocery store bag, and the bag was stored in his apartment, without ceremony. I suppose that Mom, my grandmother Yetta, kept the letters for the first forty years, because I found Russian cross-stitch embroidery patterns tucked between them; but Pop cared for them for another twenty-five years after she passed away. He knew they were important.

My parents, Sarah and Barney Moss found the letters in Pop's apartment after he died in 1970. They went there to organize his things, and my father put the letters, along with photos and other personal memorabilia, into some boxes, which he brought to our house. My Uncle Sam was encouraged to come to see what was there and to take any items he chose; but when Sam died in 1996, the collection in the boxes was still intact. That's when I was invited to choose anything that I wanted.

I found two black- and tan-colored photographic portraits on canvas, with no indication of who the subjects were. It was noted on them that they were a gift from Joe Passman, but that name meant nothing to us. I was excited when I figured out that I had found pictures of my grandparents taken at the time of their wedding. I compared Pop's picture with a much later one, and the shape of his ears was identical. Mom's distinctive hairline had never changed, and it was the same in photos from the 1930s. A final comparison with a portrait of my mother at a similar age sealed the deal!

The bag of letters was among the framed testimonial certificates and photograph albums from family events. I asked my mother if she had any idea what they might be, but she had never seen them before. Postmarks on the envelopes dated them, and I thought they were in Yiddish. Eventually my father underwrote Mark Alsher's excellent translation and, one by one, the contents were revealed to us.

The letters speak for themselves. They were written between 1904 and 1906; they were sent from Russia and America, and were written in Yiddish, Russian and Hebrew, to children, siblings, and lovers. They let us hear our ancestors' voices as they shared their lives with each other. These were private letters and no one expected us to be reading them 100 years after they were written. We live in a world of constant communication, social networking, and blogging. We have cell phones, we text, we email; we are instantly connected.

They wrote letters.

Reading someone else's letters isn't quite the same as reading a good novel from the beginning. There's not much in terms of local color, and in this case, the letters are definitely "period pieces." It's more like starting in the middle of the story and not knowing the characters or the plot so far, and you want to jump in and ask who is writing and what exactly is going on.

The photographs offer some sense of the sitters, but the clothing and formal pose hide them again. There is a stiffness in a studio portrait that is deceptive; the black and white photographic film required stillness during a long exposure. An example of this is our sole picture of Rabbi Benjamin Korman, which has the look of a patriarch, an old-world elderly sage. Now, when I look at it closely, I guess that he was under fifty years of age at the time, and that his long beard was blond, rather than gray.

I always thought of Pop as old because he was about 65 when I was born, and of course he was my grandfather. He was always dignified. He smiled, he chuckled, and he seemed interested in us. He would gather the youngest grand-children and give us money; one dollar was to be given directly to a parent to be put into "the bank" for saving, but an additional dime was for spending. We saw him often on Sundays for dinner at the country club,[1] where he always ate kosher fish, and after dinner, he often came to our house for an evening of watching TV before my father drove him home. He smoked a cigar and enjoyed a glass of schnapps, a whisky. Sometimes he sang snatches of melodies that were like the wordless "Daidle deedle daidle, did-guh, did-guh, deedle daidle dum" refrains in the songs from *Fiddler on the Roof*.[2] He never talked about himself, and he never talked about his youth in Russia.

Of course every family has stories, and each story is special. We are fortunate to have letters, first-person accounts of our family's experience during a period in history when there was upheaval and change. Perhaps what makes these letters so special is that they are not terribly unique, and that they represent the experi-ences of a whole generation of immigrants from Eastern Europe. Anti-Semitism and revolution led to violence and fear in the towns. Parents were faced with farewells to children they might never see again, and families tried to anticipate new beginnings in a foreign, and faraway, country. And still, young people met and fell in love.

I had heard bits and pieces of family lore from my parents. The letters confirm the tales and put the history into a personal context. I had never imagined Pop as romantic. I never heard him express his gratitude to live as a free American. I never knew my grandmother—for whom I am named—or my grandparents' extended families. These letters are our introduction to them and their world.

Yetta Yesersky Korman

Hyman Korman
Above: photographs found in the box.

Sarah Korman, 1935, and her father Hyman

A BRIEF FAMILY TREE

The Kormans from Brest

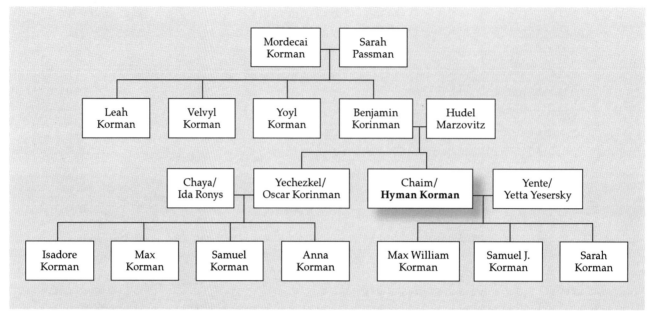

The Yeserskys from Svisloch

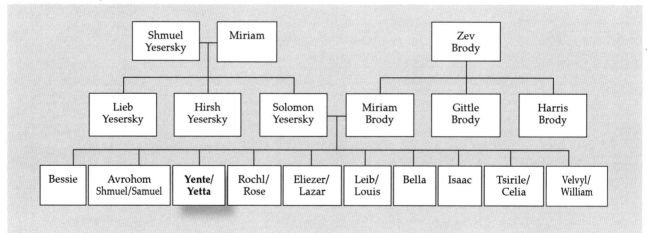

THE OLD COUNTRY

The letters were written in a world that no longer exists. A century of change the world over would have made a difference to the way Jews lived in Russia, but the Holocaust essentially destroyed all Jewish life in Eastern Europe. Whole communities were exterminated, and there are now hardly any traces. JewishGen[3] organizes tours for "shtetl schleppers,"[4] people who are looking for their roots in the towns where their families lived for generations. They often feel fortunate to find even an intact cemetery, because the Jews are gone.

When I was a child I wondered what could have made someone move from his or her home to another part of the world. As far as I knew, my entire family was in the Philadelphia area, and moving away from family and friends was inconceivable to me. I understood why the Jews of Europe did not want to leave. Ironically, I was one of the few in our family who left Philadelphia and started a life in another country when I moved to Toronto, where my husband lived. I am away, but not disconnected, because I am able to stay in touch and make frequent visits.

Our ancestors left their homes for a new start and never returned. They reinvented themselves; they changed their citizenship, their language, their customs, and even their names. I want to explain why two million of the Jews of Russia felt compelled to leave and never wanted to go back, even for a visit. This requires some Russian history and terms that may be unfamiliar, like "shtetl," "pogrom," and "the Pale of Settlement." Understanding the history and culture of that time makes it easier to understand the letters. Reading about the history makes me wonder why they didn't leave earlier.

Jewish life

Our families lived in Imperial Russia. My father told me that we were Litvaks, so I thought we were from Lithuania, and some in the family thought we were from Poland. We were and we weren't. There had once been a Grand Duchy of Lithuania (a commonwealth shared by Lithuania and Poland that existed between 1569 and 1792), which spread across a large area of what is now Lithuania, Poland, Ukraine, and Belarus, so we were geographically Litvaks.[5] At the turn of the twentieth century they lived in Grodno Gubernia, a province in Russia, part of the Pale of Settlement.[6] After World War I, our families' shtetls became Polish and later Soviet Russian. Now they are in Belarus.

Irving Howe, in his book *World of Our Fathers*, described the essence of Russian Jewish life:

> For several hundred years this culture had flourished in eastern Europe. Bound together by firm spiritual ties, by a common language, the Jews of eastern Europe were a kind of nation yet without recognized nationhood. Theirs was both a community and a society: internally a community, a ragged kingdom of the spirit, and externally a society, impoverished and imperiled.[7]

I and the Village, Marc Chagall, 1911.

No, we are not related to Chagall. I included this image because he is one of the outstanding Jewish artists of the period. Chagall (originally Shagal) was born in Russia in 1887. He became known for his fantasy paintings, which recalled his early shtetl life. Some of these paintings include images of flying brides, and the fiddler on the roof, made famous in the Broadway play of the same name. He began his study of art in Russia, but also spent time in Paris in the years before WWI. He had been arrested in 1910 for living in St. Petersburg without the permit required for Jews. Chagall returned to Russia and was a strong supporter of the 1917 Russian Revolution. He left Russia permanently in 1922 to live in Paris because he could not succeed as a Jewish modernist painter in Stalinist Russia.

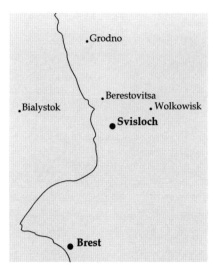

Above: The present border between Poland on the left and Belarus on the right.

Right: The Pale of Settlement which existed from 1792–1917.

The Talmud is the collection of ancient Jewish writings that forms the basis of Jewish religious law, and consists of the early scriptural interpretations and the later commentaries on them.

Orthodox Judaism was central to their being. Heaven was a real place, and prayer each day brought one closer to the time of the Messiah. Beauty was found in deeds rather than things. The carving of the Holy Arks, embroidery of a prayer shawl and calligraphy of the Holy Scripts were not separate aesthetic acts; each was integral to the cultivation of God's word.[8] A scholarly life was admired and many women became breadwinners so that their husbands could spend the day in prayer and study. People felt it a duty and privilege to support family members studying Talmud.

It was also an extremely formalized society. There are 613 mitzvot, or commandments, that an observant Jew must obey, and these describe everything in life from the way Shabbat is to be observed to the prohibition that a person must not eat or drink like a glutton or drunkard. The community was more important than the individual. They thought of themselves as the Chosen People but they lived lives of persecution, often in hopeless poverty.[9]

Even Jewish poverty had a quality that was different from the poverty of the Russian peasants, who were at least allowed to own a piece of land and feel that they might improve their lives. Most Jews were caught in poverty that was handed down from generation to generation as long as they remained as an alien people in Russia.[10] For many of them it was the hopelessness of being stuck and unable to rise above the level proscribed by the government that made people dream of the freedoms in other countries. But a Jew leaving Russia felt as if he or she was leaving the Jewish world forever.

There was, of course, a group of financially successful Jews. For example: "Jews were the key ingredient in the Ukraine's development. Management of much of the agricultural economy, administration of the nobles' lands, organization of export and import, mining and quarrying, flour milling, alcohol production and sale, were either entirely or mainly in the hands of the Yiddish-speaking community, who ensured their control by subcontracting only to their relatives and co-religionists."[11]

The emotional comfort in living in a Jewish world is expressed by the Yiddish author Sholem (Solomon) Rabinowitz, best known as Sholem Aleichem, who placed his stories in the shtetls of Eastern Europe. The majority of us are most familiar with his stories about Tevye the milkman, which formed the basis of the Broadway musical *Fiddler on the Roof*. Sometimes referred to as the Jewish Mark Twain, his writing is considered to be authentically representative of Jewish life at the turn of the century. In his introduction to a collection of Aleichem's stories, Alfred Kazin wrote:

> This is the great thing about the Jews in this book. They enjoy being Jews, they enjoy the idea of belonging to the people who are called Jews—and "their" Sholem Aleichem, perhaps more than any other Jewish writer who has ever lived, writes about Jewishness as if it were a gift, a marvel, an unending theme of wonder and delight .... The secret of this enjoyment consists not so much in physical solidarity and "togetherness," as in the absence of loneliness, as in the fact that a deep part of your life is lived below the usual level of strain, of the struggle for values, of the pressing and harrowing need—so often felt in America—to define your values all over again in each situation, where you may have even to insist on values themselves in the teeth of brutish materialism.[12]

Centuries of anti-Semitism made life in Russia impossible. It wasn't only condoned; in fact it was the official policy of the government. Jews were forced to live in towns known as "shtetls." These were small towns rather than villages; Jews were not permitted to live in villages because there was a fear that they would both influence the resident peasants as well as compete with them financially.

"Pogrom" is a Russian term originally meaning "riot."[13] It eventually was understood to mean mob violence against the Jews, and the shtetl lived in constant expectation of attack.[14] The periods around Christian holidays were especially explosive, as the government organized the clergy to preach anti-Semitism to their churchgoers. The government was a totally backward, feudal, and highly corrupt regime.[15] It was easy and convenient to blame economic problems on the Jews and encourage the masses to vent their rage and frustration by rioting in the shtetls. Frenzied mobs of Russians murdered and raped and destroyed Jewish property. It was all the more terrifying because these were random, unprovoked atrocities. Often these mobs were led by Cossacks, men who were in a local militia, and while they may not have been acting officially, their crimes were rarely punished.[16]

Mary Antin, in her memoir *The Promised Land*, described her childhood in the Russian shtetl Polotsk:

> ... the Gentiles made the Passover a time of horror for the Jews. Somebody would start up that lie about murdering Christian children, and the stupid peasants would get mad about it, and fill themselves with

Sholem Aleichem (1859–1916) was born near Kiev, but left Russia in 1904 due to the pogroms. When he died, his funeral was one of the largest in New York City history, with an estimated 100,000 mourners. His will contained detailed instructions to his family and friends, both with regard to immediate burial arrangements, as well as how he wished to be commemorated and remembered on his annual yartzheit. He told his friends and family to gather, "read my will, and also select one of my stories, one of the very merry ones, and recite it in whatever language is most intelligible to you ... Let my name be recalled with laughter," he added, "or not at all." The gatherings continue to the present day, and in recent years, have become open to the public.

This short passage is from Sholem Aleichem's An Early Passover.

Pinhas Pincus is of less than normal height, with one small eye and one bigger eye. When he talks, it seems as if the eyes talk to each other; the smaller eye asks for and seeks approval from the bigger eye; and the bigger eye gives its approval of every plan or undertaking. When he first came to Nuremberg, there was no limit to his sufferings; he had to endure starvation, misery and personal insults from his German brethren. In Nuremberg he was protected from massacres, but was not protected from starvation.

Mary Antin (Mashke) and sister Fetchke, as young children in Russia, about 1885.

Mary Antin (June 13, 1881–May 15, 1949) was an American author and immigration rights activist. Born to a Jewish family in Polotsk, Russia, she immigrated to the Boston area with her mother and siblings in 1894. She later moved to New York City where she attended Teachers College of Columbia University and Barnard College. Antin is best known for her 1912 autobiography The Promised Land, *which describes her assimilation into American culture.*

vodka, and set out to kill the Jews. They attacked them with knives and clubs and scythes and axes, killed them or tortured them, and burned their houses. This was called a "pogrom." Jews who escaped the pogroms came to Polotzk with wounds on them, and horrible, horrible stories, of little babies torn limb from limb before their mothers' eyes. Only to hear these things made one sob and sob and choke with pain. People who saw such things never smiled any more, no matter how long they lived; and sometimes their hair turned white in a day, some people became insane on the spot.[17]

Megillah Benedictions and Illuminations, painting on parchment, Italy, eighteenth century. *Library of Congress, Hebraic Section.*

But life in the shtetl went on even after a pogrom. People repaired their property and did their best to repair their lives. The shtetl was a community and it had developed according to need rather than city planning. Sometimes there were cobbled streets and occasionally there were imposing buildings such as train stations, but the shtetl was rarely pretty[18] and did not look like Boris Aronson's stage set for *Fiddler on the Roof*. Most buildings were of wood, including wooden synagogues. Perhaps one would find a few privately owned stone houses. There was usually a central marketplace with a public well for drinking water. Laws limited the Jews' choice of work so they were frequently traders or artisans. While there were no expressed social classes in the shtetl, it was not a truly democratic community. Social level was maintained through learning, economic position, and family status and pride.[19] Scholarship elevated a family's status and manual labor was often considered a mark of social disgrace.[20]

One of the positive effects of hundreds of years of restrictions was an intensification of Jewish community life and a high point of Jewish study and Talmudic scholarship. "Jewish children with musical or artistic talent could study at academies outside the Pale. Their parents and families could live with them. This greatly stimulated Jewish artistic activity over three generations and led to a flowering of Russian Jewish cultural life."[21] Charity (*tzedakah*, Hebrew for "justice") thrived and the Jews devised social welfare systems to assist their poor. "Among the charitable societies organized by Jews were those to supply poor students with clothes, soldiers with kosher food, the poor with free medical treatment, poor brides with dowries, and orphans with technical education."[22] Rabbi Ken Spiro wrote:

> This caring for each other did not escape the notice of non-Jews. In fact, during this period of time the rabbis had to issue a decree against accepting any converts to Judaism from the local Slavic population. Why would Christian Slavs want to convert to Judaism? They realized that no Jew ever starved to death in the street, whereas if you were a Christian peasant you could easily starve to death in the street because no one was going to take care of you. The government wasn't going to do it and the Church wasn't going to do it. So the rabbis didn't want Judaism being flooded by thousands of insincere converts who were trying to save their lives by becoming Jews and benefiting from the Jewish welfare system.[23]

The rabbinical reluctance to accept converts was probably the only Jewish attitude that really pleased the government of Russia!

Ketubbah, Madallena on the Po, 1839. The double archway decorating this ketubbah is surrounded by birds and flowers. The words in the banner held in the birds' beaks read, "He who has found a wife has found virtue." *Library of Congress, Hebraic Collection.*

Strasse in Slonim

A street in Slonim, a typical shtetl scene in Grodno Gubernia, about 1900. *Postcard courtesy of Adrian Andrusier.*

Yicchus, *meaning "status," is a very important word in Jewish culture. It is a word that is perhaps more than a thousand years old and may have been rooted in family genealogies and scholarship. It grew to reflect upper class occupations; and we are all familiar with the proud phrase, "my son the doctor."* Yicchus *is also a reflection of material wealth. A person can gain* yicchus *through the recognition of charitable gifts, and it is the concept behind the success of the charity "ad book" and the publication of an individual's levels of donation to various Jewish causes.*

Our Shtetls

Mukhavets River, Brest, 2007. *Photograph by Henry Neugass.*

Brest

Shosseinaya Street.

The market in Brest, about 1900.

A postcard of Brest, along the river, 1900.

The Kormans were also the Korinmans, and I have not been able to discover why the family used two names within the same generation. Chaim Korman and Yehezkel Korinman were brothers. They lived in Brest, Grodno Gubernia, also known by its Yiddish name Brisk, and by Brest-Litovsk, Brisk D'lita, and several other names that refer to the fact that it was once in The Grand Dutchy of Lithuania. It is situated where the Western Bug and Mukhavets Rivers meet and, because of its location, has a strong military history.

There were already Jews settled in Brest in 1388, when they were granted a charter by the Grand Duke Vitautas of Lithuania to live there. Brest contained a synagogue which was founded in 1411 and was regarded in the 16th century as the first in the Grand Dutchy of Lithuania.[24] In 1897, the Jewish population of Brest was 30,252, 65% of a total population of 46,568. People who lived there often called themselves Briskers.[25]

In Brest in the early 1900s, the Jews controlled most of the trade and industries, such as tobacco, liquor, salt, timber, and matches but mostly people worked in the same sort of jobs they would have done in a city like Philadelphia.[26] They ran the local shops, and the tradesmen, such as tailors, bakers, butchers, shoemakers, and photographers, supplied both the townspeople and the peasants from the surrounding villages. By 1890, the railroad connected Brest with Warsaw, Moscow, and other industrial centers, and a grand railway station was built in the city in 1886.[27]

Brest suffered through two great fires; the first in 1895 destroyed one-half of the city, and the second in 1901, destroyed the second half. Jews abroad were moved to send donations, and even Czar Nicholas II gave 300,000 rubles to aid the victims.[28] The city had been built mainly of wood but after the fires, brick houses appeared, and their numbers soon increased.

Chaya Korinman's sister Bella with her children, Sidney and Arthur, in front of their house in Brest. *Photograph courtesy of Goldie Seiderman.*

Some public buildings of the time have survived a century of wear, architectural fashions, and the world wars, and are still in use. The town included two public parks and about 35 streets (about 40 % paved), and there was also a large central market. But before WWII, at least 90% of the Jewish homes had no running water or indoor toilets. The city's boundary line was made up of railway lines, the river, and the Brest Fortress. The Brest Fortress was built between 1836 and 1842 with new stone walls replacing the remains of a castle which had been built in the 13th century.[29] Although the modern fortress became a significant fortification on the Russian border,[30] the German Army captured the town in August 1915. The 1918 Treaty of Brest-Litovsk ended Russia's involvement in WWI.

Russian map of the city of Brest, 1914.

The beautiful synagogue in the center of Brest had been converted to a cinema many years ago. The lower picture shows the most recent renovation that was completed in 2008. *Photograph courtesy of city-walk.brest-belarus.org.*

Brest Railway Station. *Photograph courtesy of city-walk.brest-belarus.org.*

Top postcard: Faivel Synagogue. *Courtesy of Adrian Andrusier.* Bottom: The same building in 2008. The building was reduced to its walls and the decorative details were destroyed during World War I. *Photograph by Oleg Medvedevsky of city-walk. brest-belarus.org.*

Painting of Brest Street, Svisloch, by Napoleon Orda, late 19th century.
Courtesy of Deborah Glassman.

Svisloch

There are two Svisloch shtetls, which leads to confusion. "Our" Svisloch was in Grodno Gubernia and the other was in Minsk Gubernia where Napoleon Orda, the artist, was born. The painting shown above may be of the Svisloch where he attended secondary school, but as there is a Brisker, or Brest, Street in each Svisloch, I cannot say which Svisloch is in his painting. Clearly, I would like to claim it! I think it is fair to say that this lovely work illustrates a town typical of the mid-19th century.

The synagogue yard was the courtyard of the synagogue. It was called the shulhoyf *and was the spiritual and social center of the shtetl. It was the place to celebrate weddings and other ceremonies and festivals, and often had a yeshiva (a Jewish school of higher learning) attached to it.*

The Yeserskys (Yeserski, Jezierski) lived in Svisloch (Swislocz, Swislacs, and Sislevich in Yiddish). The pronunciation is "Svees-lud-cje." Although it was much smaller than Brest—3000 people in Svisloch vs. 45,000 in Brest—it was still considered one of the larger towns in Wolkowysk district, also in Grodno Gubernia, and "typical of the larger, more urbanized shtetlach."[31] Surrounded by flat farmland and marshy areas along the Svisloch River, Svisloch enjoyed a climate similar to Philadelphia's. When the railway was built at the beginning of the 1900s, Svisloch became linked with industrial centers in Western Russia and many Jews and non-Jews moved to the town.[32] There were about 2000 Jews, about two-thirds of the population.[33]

The details of the early history of Svisloch were lost. Abraham Ain recalled:

The Holy Burial Association (Khevre Kadishe) formerly had a pinkes, a minute-book, but it was destroyed in one of the periodic fires, and no other source for the history of the Jews in town was left.

The Jewish cemetery was divided into a new and an old burial ground. On the old cemetery, near the entrance, the tombstones had collapsed, so that it was difficult to tell that the place had once been a burial ground. Farther down, the tombstones protruded half-way from the ground, but the inscriptions on them were obliterated. On the new cemetery the graves and tombstones were in better condition. But even the new cemetery had probably been used for centuries, for in the first World War it was filled up and ground was broken for another cemetery.[34]

The town consisted of a market, five large and a dozen small streets and alleys, and a synagogue yard. Many of the larger homes were multistory brick residences. Most of the streets were unpaved but there were sidewalks around the central market square. The market covered an area of about two city blocks in the center of the town and all of the towns businesses, about 60, were housed there.[35] All of the larger streets, which extended on the average to three or four city blocks, began in the market and terminated in the fringes. These streets—Grodno Street, Warsaw Street, Brisker Street—were named after the towns to which they led.[36] The post office was on Amstibover Street.

Svisloch was surrounded by many small villages and the Jews in town provided the farmers with many of the items they needed. The major economic enterprises in the town were the eight leather factories, as well as a dozen small shops, which together employed more than 400 workers. The Jews built the tanning factories in the 1870s with the assistance of German master craftsmen who they invited to Svisloch. By 1900, all the skilled workers were Jews.[37]

An elected community council administered all religious and community affairs. The council paid the salaries of the rabbi and other functionaries and maintained the ritual bathhouse and the poorhouse. The money for these activities came from a tax on kosher meat and slaughter.[38]

The economic situation of the town was moderately good; the people were well-fed and well-dressed. But it's difficult to imagine a place with sanitary conditions as primitive as Svisloch, where some homes did not even have outhouses and people met their needs in the open. Water had to be pumped from community wells, which were not covered and collected dust and dirt. There was a single community bathhouse that was badly overcrowded in winter. Conditions were better in the summer because then some people bathed in the river.[39]

One physician served the municipal hospital; he had one assistant and a midwife. The Jews generally avoided the hospital, although they sometimes saw the physician or his assistant as private patients. There were also two Polish physicians, one Jewish assistant and two Jewish midwives in private practice.[40]

Svisloch had ties with Bialystok, 45 miles to the west; among other things, it was the place to buy goods that were not available in Svisloch. Bialystok is now part of Poland. Grodno, to the north, was the other large town near Svisloch. The completion of the railway line in 1906 expanded Svisloch's commercial ties to the town of Wolkowysk, about 19 miles to the northeast, where Solomon Yesersky was born.

I have tried to visualize Svisloch in the early 1900s. Transportation was by horsepower and Solomon's stagecoach line, as well as private carriages and wagons, depended on these animals. In a large city you would have heard the sharp sound of horseshoes striking pavement, but Svisloch had streets made of packed earth. In the early spring, when the frost was coming out of the ground and before the soil dried out, the roads must have been mushy and difficult. Abraham Ain remarked that on rainy days the streets around the market were ankle-deep in mud.

The main industry was tanning leather, and the pungent smell of that process must have spread through town on a warm day.

From photographs, we can see how the people dressed during the early 1900s. But to create a better picture of how they really lived, I have included some information on the next few pages about the food that was typically eaten in Svisloch since so much of Jewish family life involves eating together. There is a bit of truth in the quip that sums up the Jewish historical celebration: "They tried to destroy us; God saved us; Let's eat!"

Most of us do not eat krupnik or kugel on a regular basis. Most of us have never tasted petcha, which actually tastes much better than the ingredients would lead you to suppose.

My mother told me that her mother made brisket, eggplant chopped with onion and tomato, prakes, which were cabbage leaves stuffed with ground beef and rice, and goulash, which was a beef stew mixed with home-canned mixed vegetables. In the spring they ate schav, a cold soup made from sorrel leaves, and later in the year, ate a beet borscht— both soups enriched with sour cream. I have the impression that their food was very traditional and never very improvisational.

It is said that every Jewish recipe begins with the instructions: "Fry an onion." Every recipe. Why? Because it makes the house smell so good!

Food in Svisloch

Like every other town, Swislocz, too, had a nickname: Sislevicher krupnik. The town fully deserved that nickname. For there was not a day, except the Sabbath and the holidays, when krupnik was not on the menu of every Jewish home in town. What is krupnik? It is a thick soup of barley or groats mixed with potatoes. In the winter time, when meat was cheap, a slice of lamb or veal was added to the mixture. In the summer time, when meat was expensive, only the wealthy could afford to season their krupnik with meat. Most people had to be content with a little beef fat in their krupnik, to which onions were added as a preservative.

For the Friday breakfast the krupnik was prepared differently, as a rule with stuffed gut. It was eaten with fresh rolls, which nearly all Jewish women baked on Friday.

Friday was also graced with potato pudding. Advantage was taken of the fact that the oven was kindled for the baking of Sabbath bread (challah). Some families had potato pudding twice on Friday. Another popular dish was lekshlekh bulve, peeled potatoes, thinly sliced and boiled with meat. The dish was prepared in the morning, placed in the oven, and eaten for lunch or for supper. Likewise popular were potatoes boiled in their jackets (sholekhts bulve). The wealthy ate the potatoes with herring; the rest, with herring sauce. On the whole, potatoes were a staple in the diet of our district, both among Jews and non-Jews. It was not without a measure of justification that the district of Grodno was known in Russia as "the Grodno potato."

From "Swislocz: Portrait of a Shtetl," by Abraham Ain. Reprinted with permission of YIVO Institute for Jewish Research, New York.

Krupnik/ Mushroom Barley Soup

Serves 10

This soup is traditionally prepared with dried mushrooms. In Eastern Europe the mushrooms were gathered in the wild and dried over the stove. The dried mushrooms were stored in jars and a supply was accumulated to last through the winter.

This version of the soup has many vegetables but it can be made with only the mushrooms and barley.

- 1 ½ oz. dried mushrooms
- 12 cups of water or stock
- 2 small carrots
- 2 small turnips
- 2 small onions
- 2 medium potatoes
- 2 celery stalks and their leaves
- ¾ cup pearl barley
- Salt and pepper

Soak the mushrooms in a little hot water for about 15 minutes to soften them. The mushrooms should be removed from the soaking liquid and the liquid strained to remove any sand or dirt.

The vegetables and mushrooms can be chopped in a food processor or diced by hand.

Add all of the ingredients and the soaking liquid, except the barley, to a large pot. Bring to a boil and remove the scum. Season well with salt and pepper and add the barley. Simmer 1 hour or until the barley is very soft. Add more water if the soup becomes too thick.

Potato Kugel/ Potato Pudding

Serves 6

Claudia Roden, in *The Book of Jewish Food*, begins her kugel recipe with the following anecdote:

"In 1825, the German poet Heinrich Heine wrote in a letter to the editor of a Jewish magazine, 'Kugel, this holy national dish, has done more for the preservation of Judaism than all three issues of this magazine.'"

Sometimes kugel is made from mashed potatoes, but this traditional recipe, using grated potatoes, has a nicer texture. Its taste, as well as its ingredients, are very similar to potato latkes.

2 eggs

1 ½ teaspoons salt

¼ teaspoon pepper

¼ cup vegetable oil or chicken fat (*schmaltz*)

1 large onion grated

6 medium size potatoes, peeled

In a bowl, beat the eggs adding the salt and pepper, the oil, and the onion.

Grate the potatoes quickly so they do not discolor. Put them into a colander and squeeze out the excess liquid by pressing with your hands or a large spoon. Add the potatoes to the egg mixture.

Pour the mixture into a wide, shallow baking dish so that there will be a lot of crispy crust after it is baked. Bake at 350° F for about 1 hour, or until brown. Serve hot.

Chicken Soup

Serves 6

Bessie Yesersky's recipe, shared by her daughter Fannye Taylor

3 pounds kosher chicken

3 quarts cold water

3 large carrots, cut into 2" chunks

3 large celery stalks, cut into 2" chunks

1 large onion

1 medium sweet potato

Salt and pepper

Fresh parsnip and dill (called soup greens) tied together and wrapped in cheesecloth

Bring chicken and water to a boil. Gradually skim foam. Simmer 30 minutes.

Add vegetables, except soup greens. Cook 30 minutes.

Add soup greens. Cook 15 minutes more. Remove soup greens, onion, and potato.

Season with salt and pepper. Serve soup with chicken which may be removed from the bone.

Petcha/ Calf's Foot Jelly

Serves 6

The most difficult part of making petcha is locating a calf's foot. Petcha is really aspic, and aspics have mostly fallen out of fashion. That's too bad because it tastes good and it is not slimy. It's the meat version of the jelly around gefilte fish but much firmer.

1 calf's foot, cut into several pieces

1 onion

2 cloves garlic

1 bay leaf

Juice of 1 lemon

2 tablespoons cider vinegar

1 teaspoon salt

1/2 teaspoon peppercorns

2 eggs, hard-boiled

Wash and blanch the calf's foot. Cover it with cold water and bring to a boil. Simmer 5–10 minutes and pour out the water when the scum forms.

Cover the feet again with fresh cold water. Cook 2 hours. Add the onion, garlic, bay leaf, lemon juice, and vinegar, and cook 1 hour longer. The meat and cartilage should be very soft and come away from the bone.

Cut the meat into small pieces and place in a deep dish. Strain the liquid over the meat. Add the sliced eggs. Chill overnight or until jellied and firm. Serve the petcha cut into squares or slices. Pickles are a nice accompaniment.

The Historical Context of Imperial Russia:
The Czars and the Jews

Catherine II, ruled 1762–1796

Catherine the Great and the Pale of Settlement

Catherine II was called "Great" because her rule was one of the most prosperous periods of the Russian Empire.[41] Catherine increased the power and prestige of Russia by skillful diplomacy and by extending Russia's western boundary into central Europe.[42] Greatness did not extend to her attitude about the Jews.

Catherine devised the Pale of Settlement in 1792 as a way to manage the very large population of Polish Jews who lived in the areas that had recently been annexed by Russia. She found her new subjects to be very foreign and distasteful and the Pale of Settlement, which meant "borders of settlement," was a way to physically contain the Jews. The Pale became the only area of Russia where the Jews were permitted to live and work, and creating it also forced the Jews to move out of St. Petersburg and Moscow because she thought "tolerance of other religions might bring about disloyalty to the supreme truth of Christianity."[43]

Eventually, the area of the Pale was expanded, partly as a result of further annexations, but even within the Pale, the Jews were subjected to many restrictions.[44] Subsequent Czars made the legal restrictions harsher still and it took the Russian Revolution of 1917 to abolish both the laws and the position of Czar.

Nicholas I, ruled 1825–1855

Nicholas I and the Cantonist Decrees

Jews did not have all the rights of other Russian citizens, but they were not exempt from taxation and military service in the Russian Army. In 1827, Czar Nicholas I (who ruled from 1825 to 1855) introduced what became known as the Cantonist Decrees. The name came from the word "canton," meaning "military camp." The law fixed the rate of Jewish conscription at a rate 40% percent higher than that of non-Jews.[45]

Cantonist schools were formed and Jewish boys of 8 to 10 years were taken from their family homes and forced to enroll.[46] Unattended boys were often kidnapped to satisfy the quotas set by the government.[47] These boys were trained in military schools and at 18 they were forced into the army to serve for 25 years.

Due to the horrendous conditions under which they were forced to serve, very few of the boys who were conscripted came out alive. It was army policy to attempt to convert the soldiers to Christianity so that if they did survive they no longer identified themselves as Jews.[48] They were often given new Russian names.[49] "They were taken as far from their birthplace as possible. Those mobilized at Kiev were sent to Perm, over 1000 miles away; those at Brest to Nizhniy-Novgorod, not much less a distance."[50] "As far as the Jewish community was concerned, either way was a death sentence."[51]

"Some families were able to buy their son's way out of the conscription, but most were extremely poor. The cost of buying one's self out of the army was even greater than the cost of a steerage ticket to England or the USA. When the emigrant attempted to send money 'back home' to help pay these fines, the letters were frequently opened by the post office authorities to search for money orders or cash, and the money seldom reached the families most in need of it."[52]

There were Jewish parents so desperate they would actually cut off the right index fingers of their sons with butcher's knives—without an index finger you couldn't fire a gun and you were exempt from service. Young men literally "shot themselves in the foot" rather than be conscripted. Many just ran away or deserted.[53]

General censorship had been in force in Russia since 1826, but Nicholas I felt that the Jews needed extra censorship. On October 27, 1836, a ministerial committee decided to close all existing Hebrew printing presses, except two—one in Kiev and the other in Vilna.

The Boy Soldiers

In his memoirs, My Past and Thoughts, *Alexander Herzen, the Russian historian, unforgettably portrayed a convoy of conscripted Jewish children. In the mid 1830s he wrote:*

"You see, they have collected a crowd of cursed little Jewish boys of eight or nine years old" [a Russian officer tells Herzen in a village in the province of Vyata]."… they just die off like flies. A Jew boy, you know, is such a frail, weakly creature … he is not used to tramping in the mud for ten hours a day and eating biscuit … being among strangers, no father nor mother nor petting; well, they cough and cough until they cough themselves into their graves."

… it was one of the most awful sights I have ever seen, those poor, poor children! Boys of twelve or thirteen might somehow have survived it, but little fellows of eight or ten …

Pale, exhausted, with frightened faces, they stood in thick, clumsy, soldiers' overcoats, with stand up collars, fixing helpless, pitiful eyes on the garrison soldiers who were roughly getting them into ranks. The white lips, the blue rings under the eyes looked like fever or chill and these sick children, without care or kindness, exposed to the icy wind that blows unobstructed from the Arctic Ocean, were going to their graves.

During the Crimean War (1853–1856)"the million-man Russian army was filled out with rail-thin, vodka-sotted conscripts, who—conscripted for an astonishing twenty-five years of service—died of exhaustion and disease at twice the rate of the French or British armies. Like the Royal Navy, the Russian fleet used pressgangs [coerced or forced enlistees] to man its ships, relying for the most part on Jewish boys seized from the wretched shtetls of Belarus, Poland, and Ukraine. In the 1850s, fully one-third of the Russian sailors were Jewish, a curious statistic. The mortality rate in the navy was even higher than in the army, which explained the institution of the 'crippler' in the Russian village: a hired thug who would cut off toes or fingers of peasant boys or smash out their teeth to render them unfit for military service."
Geoffrey Wawro. *Warfare and Society in Europe, 1792–1914.*

"In 1902 a list of Jews who avoided military service (e.g. because of emigration to the USA) was published in the Latvian newspaper Kurlandskiye gubernskiye vedomosti *[KGV]. The relatives who remained in Russia were forced to pay 'the enormous pain in 300 rubles' In KGV the authorities announced they were searching for the members of the family of the person who had avoided military service (in 1901), and published the names of the relatives and their ages, including the draft avoider's parents and brother, and searched their property, asking for payment in the amount of 300 rubles. So it would seem that 300 rubles was the standard fine to be paid by the family for draft evasion for the early part of the 20th Century at least. This applied to families within the entire Pale of Settlement."*
Davida Handler, et al. "Revision Lists"

Alexander II, ruled 1855–1881

Alexander II

Benjamin Disraeli, the British Prime Minister, called Alexander II "the kindliest prince who has ever ruled Russia," but that only meant that he was relatively benign compared to the others. Alexander II was one of the more competent czars, and he reduced the period of military service to five years, allowed some Jews into the universities, and permitted some businessmen to travel beyond the Pale.[54]

He also freed the 40 million serfs of Russia who had been legally tied to the land. Unfortunately his emancipation of the serfs half ruined the landowners while creating a free but penniless peasantry. The properties the former serfs received were often too small to support their families and often freed serfs were given land that was not arable.

The Jews had not been serfs and could be neither nobles nor peasants. Prohibited from owning farmland, some Jews found a vocation as moneylenders and as middlemen between the farming grain producers and the grain consumers and exporters.

In 1881 Alexander II was assassinated by a revolutionary, who was rumored to have been part of a Jewish plot.[55] This rumor set off waves of pogroms across the Pale of Settlement. The Russian economy was still in a terrible state and when the problems of Russia got worse, the problems of the Jews got worse as well. [56]

Alexander III, ruled 1881–1894

Alexander III and the May Laws

The government of the new czar, Alexander III (who ruled from 1881 to 1894), organized one pogrom after another to keep the anger of the masses focused on the Jews rather than on the government. In May, 1882, Alexander III also declared a new series of "temporary" restrictive laws against the Jews which lasted for 30 years, until the Russian Revolution of 1917. These laws were called the May Laws, and in 1890 the *London Daily News* printed an article, "A Russian Jew's Story," containing a letter which had been written to a London rabbi with the hope of some help from the English Jews in the form of "substance, wisdom, and advocacy." This article was reprinted in the *New York Times* as well as the *Daily Critic* in Washington, D.C. The Russian Jewish writer describes the May laws which he says will "deprive us of our livelihood in those parts of the country in which we have been hitherto allowed to reside:"

1. No Jew may leave the town for the purpose of residing in the country.
2. No Christian is allowed to let land to a Jew.
3. No Jew may keep an inn or sell intoxicants in any part of the country.
4. A Jew settled in a country place before 1882 may reside there until his lease expires, but he may not leave his village. If he leaves the village he may not return, and may not go to any other village, but must settle in a town. All Jews settled in a village since 1882 must leave and live in a town.

5. When the lease granted to a Jew settled in a village expires it may not be renewed, but he must leave and settle in a town.

These five decrees consist of many clauses and paragraphs … For example, many townlets are by the government regarded as villages, and from these Jewish residents will be expelled. … It is intended to repeal the law of 1865 which gave artisans the right to settle in the interior of the country. This means the expulsion of 200,000. They are to be forced upon our brethren in the towns who are already crowded and crushed to the limit of their residence.

The writer continues and explains that half a million will be affected when their pre-1882 country leases expire and another half million will be affected if they settled in the country after 1882.

Alexander II had believed that Jews could be secularized with Russian education and he had commanded the Jews to attend Russian high schools and universities. The May Laws removed the Jews from the schools and prohibited them from becoming engineers, lawyers, doctors in the Army, or holding any government post. They were also dismissed from the Post Office, railways, telegraph offices, and as notaries and clerks to the governments in the towns and villages.

The writer ends his letter with a plea: "Help to preserve us and our wives and children–all of them at the gates of death and destruction."[57]

The May Laws that restricted the Jews work as financial backers turned out to be a disaster for the Russian economy. As noted in the 1910 *Encyclopaedia Britannica*:

The Russian May Laws are the most conspicuous legislative monument achieved by modern anti-Semitism. Their result was a widespread commercial depression which was felt all over the empire. Trade was everywhere paralyzed. The enormous increase of bankruptcies, the transfer of investments to foreign funds, the consequent fall in the value of the ruble and the prices of Russian stocks, the suspension of farming operations owing to advances on growing crops being no longer available, the rise in the prices of the necessaries of life, and lastly, the appearance of famine, filled half the empire with gloom. Banks closed their doors, and the great provincial fairs proved failures. When it was proposed to expel the Jews from Moscow there was a loud outcry all over the sacred city, and even the [Russian] Orthodox merchants, realizing that the measure would ruin their flourishing trade with the south and west, petitioned against it. The Moscow Exhibition proved a failure. Nevertheless the government persisted with its harsh policy, and Jewish refugees streamed by tens of thousands across the western frontier to seek asylum in other lands.[58]

Alexander III's note on a margin of a memorandum that urged curtailing repressive practices read, "But we must never forget that the Jews have crucified our Master and have shed his precious blood." Alexander's advisor acknowl-

Moneylending has negative associations and Shakespeare's Shylock has become the most famous literary example of the Jewish moneylender. Paul Kriwaczek, in his book Yiddish Civilization, *observed that it was during the Middle Ages that Jews became moneylenders. They had been farmers and shopkeepers during the rule of the Roman Empire but after the Romans' "military attack, economic collapse, disease and starvation hit the Hebraic middle and working classes disproportionately hard." Many fled to avoid starving to death and even gave up their religion and Jewish identity. But those who stayed found the advantages of becoming businessmen and many entered international trade. This led, over the following centuries, to the Jewish stereotypical involvement in banking, moneylending and exchange. "For many centuries there was no other source of finance for churchmen wanting to build cathedrals, nobles caught in financial embarrassment, merchants obliged to buy what they would then sell, even peasants needing seed for the next growing season." High rates came with high risk, but whenever the Jews were expelled (England in 1290 and France in 1395) the gentiles who replaced them raised the rates even higher. It seems that high interest rates "were a consequence of the desperately insecure financial environment rather than Jewish greed." Moneylenders were simply the forerunners of today's bankers.*

The state emblem of the Russian Empire, with a double-headed eagle.

edged that the Czar's measures were intended to destroy the Jewish community as a social and religious body and over 600 anti-Jewish decrees were enacted. It was hoped that a third of the Jews might be converted to Christianity, a third might be pushed into emigration from Russia, and a third might die.[59] In the end the Jewish problem would be solved.

Czar Alexander III's government was so out of touch with the issues of its country that the leaders had no idea that the peasants were starving during the terrible famine of 1891 in the Volga region. The May Laws had removed the Jewish moneylenders who traditionally financed the farmers so they could buy seed and plant the next crop, repaying the loans at harvest time. Then, the weather conditions caused a failure of the crop. The peasant farmers were always on the edge of poverty because emancipation had given them inadequate acreage to feed a family. They had no money for modern phosphate fertilizers and, because their region was not forested, they traditionally used manure for fire fuel rather than for fertilizer. A successful crop meant everything to the farmers and while they depended on it for food, it also provided their clothing, fuel, taxes, and fodder for the animals.

The tax collectors were the first to report the failed harvest and that the peasants could not pay. The government had the tax collectors seize the livestock and the horses, which the farmers used to till the fields, compounding the disaster. Weakened by malnutrition, desperate peasants traveled from town to town to seek work, and in doing so, they spread diseases such as scarlet fever, typhus, diphtheria, cholera, and smallpox throughout the region. The famine showed the poor standard of living and medieval conditions that the majority of the population endured. It affected about fourteen to twenty million people and about 400,000 people died from starvation and disease, their government incapable of handling a relief effort. It was a disaster that did not have to happen.[60]

Nicholas II, ruled 1894–1917

Nicholas II, Revolution and Reprisals

At the time our family letters were written, the czar was Nicolas II (he ruled from 1894 to 1917). Nicholas II did not find a way to improve the situation in Russia and the government was faced with uprisings from farmers, soldiers, and the unemployed. Perhaps Russia's expansion into the Far East was designed as a diversion: Russian military strength was a key to national pride and another Russian triumph could bolster the spirits of the population.[61] Russia had fought along with Japan in the Chinese Boxer Rebellion of 1900, but by maintaining troops in Manchuria, Russia provoked a war with Japan in 1904.

Chaim Korman, age 23, was in the Russian Army in 1904. He anticipated that his regiment in Smolensk would soon be sent to Karaol in Kazakhstan, but on July 11 he wrote to Yente that for the moment they were "not set to go to the east … but what will be later cannot be known."

Chaim made the decision to desert the army and Russia and he emigrated to

New York in December, 1904. On May 14, 1905 his father, Rabbi Korinman, wrote to him, "I also inform you that Noach, the son of Yaakov Brubin, he too fled from the army and went to New York because most of our brethren from the regiments in Smolensk were sent to the war, to the slaughterhouse."

The fabled Russian military machine proved to be inept and the Russo-Japanese War of 1904-1905 *was* a slaughterhouse and a disaster. The Army was incapable of adequate movement of the necessary numbers of troops and supplies across the vastness of Russia—cavalry soldiers were sent across the continent on horseback—although the new Trans-Siberian Railroad was almost complete. Leadership was lacking in crucial major naval battles and Japan crushed the Russian military. This failure was a terrible humiliation for the Russian government. 400,000 men were killed, wounded, or captured, and material losses were valued at 2.5-billion gold rubles.[62] The Russo-Japanese War revealed how corrupt and incompetent the Czarist regime had become and the disastrous outcome of the war for Russia became one of the immediate causes of the Russian Revolution of 1905.[63]

Czar Nicholas II was "a stubborn supporter of the right of the sovereign, despite growing pressure for revolution, and he did not give way on a single issue, even when common sense and circumstances demanded it."[64] The Russian Revolution of 1905 began in St. Petersburg on "Bloody Sunday" in January when troops fired on a defenseless crowd of workers who, led by a priest, were marching to the Winter Palace to petition Czar Nicholas II. The incident led to a series of strikes, riots, assassinations, mutinies, and peasant uprisings. The Czar struggled to hold onto absolute power, but finally he produced the Imperial Manifesto of February 18, 1905, calculated to appease the people. It called on loyal Russians to unite against their foreign and domestic foes,[65] granted civil liberties, and created an assembly that would be elected democratically.[66] Predictably, these freedoms were soon annulled.

But at the time, the Czar's concessions came with vicious action against the revolutionaries, 90% of whom the Czar himself claimed were Jewish. Once again the Jews became the Russian government's focus and more than 80% of the pogroms of 1905-1906 occurred in the 60 days following the release of the Manifesto.[67] A notorious literary forgery—a hideous pack of lies—called *The Protocols of the Elders of Zion* was circulated to defame the Jews and promote anti-Semitism. In Brest, the propaganda and hatred was spread by the Organization of King Michael (Soyuz Mikhael Arkangel),[68] which was a group named after Archangel Michael, who the Russian Orthodox Church believes has been chosen by God to defeat Satan and his evil angels.[69]

Brest was a transit station and camp for the army, and the city was full of soldiers and reservists returning from the disastrous Russo-Japanese War.[70] In many towns the pogroms were the work of policemen or soldiers, but the "excesses" of May 29, 1905 were attributed to drunken reservists.[71] On June 16, 1905 Rabbi Benjamin Korinman described this pogrom in his letter to his son Chaim:

Fighting a war in Manchuria required extraordinary manipulation of the Russian military resources. The Trans-Siberian Railroad was incomplete at Lake Baikal, the largest freshwater lake in the world. In February 1904, twenty-five miles of railroad track was built across the lake when it froze to a thickness of five feet.

The Russian navy sailed a distance equal to traveling halfway around the globe, moving from the home ports on the Baltic Sea to reach the war in Manchuria. In the end, the Russians were overpowered by the Japanese Navy and most of the Russian ships were destroyed.

Tsushima, Kiyochika (1847-1915), 1905.
This woodblock print is one in a series of humorous depictions of events of the time. Kiyochika celebrated the aftermath of the Battle of Tsushima, a turning point in the Russo-Japanese War. On May 27, 1905 the Japanese navy annihilated the Russian fleet. The picture is of the ships, wounded and bandaged with the Russian flag, limping away.

Bloody Sunday, St. Petersburg 1905. This picture may be from a propaganda film produced shortly after the event took place.

The Russian Revolution of 1905 was reported in *The Philadelphia Inquirer*, which published this cartoon by Fred Morgan. It shows the hammer of Oppression and Revolution pounding the Czar, forcing him to see stars of Liberty, Freedom, Constitution, and Parliament.

Before all discussion, I will inform you that we are all thank God alive and peaceful ... the devastations and horrors in all of the land of Russia, pogroms and pillaging and in general the Jews in Russia are in an awful situation, may the Lord have mercy on them. And also in Brisk this week there was a big pogrom in some streets, and they looted and plundered much and also some people were killed by the guns and also many were wounded, because of the reserves [the Russian soldiers of the Libava Regiment stationed in Brest], the rioters who came here by the thousands, and though at the moment the noise and tumult has quieted down, thank God, nevertheless, the city is in fear ... and almost half the people have left the city.[72]

Between 1903 and 1907, times of great internal unrest in Russia, there were 284 pogroms with over 50,000 casualties: "The level of violence was unbelievable."[73]

There had been emigration from Russia for decades; families often sent their sons away to avoid military service. The striking difference was that in this period, entire families sold everything they owned and traveled great distances to get to port cities, risking everything for the hope of a better life elsewhere. An average of 65,000 Jews left Russia each year between 1881 and 1914 when Russia entered into World War I and emigration was halted. Many went to England, Canada, Argentina, South Africa, and the Holy Land (the first four presidents of Israel were Russian-born), but the majority emigrated to America.[74]

This postcard is addressed to:
Mr. Brody
230 Greenwich Street
Philadelphia Pa. America

AMERICA

Red Star Line   Antwerpen NewYork

S. S. Zeeland. Sept. 14th 1905

Postcard of The S.S. Zeeland, operated by The Red Star Line.

The Voyage to New York

Chaim Korman arrived at Ellis Island on December 14, 1904. His ship, the S.S. Zeeland, had sailed from Antwerp eleven days earlier[75] and crossing the North Atlantic in December must have been rough. We have no letters that describe his travel experience, so I must imagine that his trip was similar to that of others who have written recollections.

His passage was in steerage, which was the least expensive class of travel, named because it was the lowest passenger deck and just above the motors. A ticket from Bremen or Antwerp cost about $31, the equivalent of about $800 in 2010. The Red Star Line, which operated the Zeeland, carried passengers from Europe to America, but on the return trip, the steerage accommodations were disassembled and the space was used for cargo. Steerage was set up like a dormitory with bunks, each six feet long and two feet wide. The washrooms were shared, often by men and women, with no regard for privacy; a separate women's section did not protect a woman from peeping toms and even assault.[76] The wash basins had only cold sea water and were used for everything from personal hygiene to washing diapers. There was no staff that cleaned the facilities during the voyage. Food was often included with the price of the ticket, but the quality was poor and if the passenger was Jewish the non-kosher food was inedible. Sometimes, a storm might literally toss people from their beds and many people seem to have been seasick the entire trip.

Statue of Liberty National Monument. *Library of Congress.*

Most of the travelers had never before seen the ocean and being out of the sight of land for so long was very frightening. They were also living with people from other countries and trying, not always successfully, to get along in multiple languages and deal with different customs. If you can imagine these close quarters

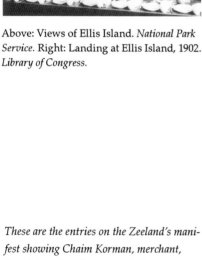

Above: Views of Ellis Island. *National Park Service.* Right: Landing at Ellis Island, 1902. *Library of Congress.*

and add filth, stench, and hunger, you have some picture of the steerage experience.

By the time the ship landed at Ellis Island, the passengers were exhausted and disoriented. They were also terribly anxious. They had heard so many rumors that they had no idea how to behave; some had heard that they should hide any money they had and tell the inspectors they had none, not knowing that they actually were expected to have some money with them. They were fearful that the doctors performing health inspections might find some reason to exclude them, or a family member, and send them back to Europe where they had nothing left.

The immigration records at Ellis Island indicate that Chaim arrived from Antwerp, Belgium. The Zeeland's manifest shows that Chaim identified himself as 23 years old, a merchant from Litowsk (Brest-Litowsk), in possession of $10 and headed for his cousin from the Passman side of the family at 209 Forsyth Street on the Lower East Side. He was fortunate to have his grandmother's relatives in New York, so he did not arrive without a place to stay, and they helped him become accustomed to American life. His family was expecting him but he certainly wasn't expecting New York.

These are the entries on the Zeeland's manifest showing Chaim Korman, merchant, from Litowsk, going to cousin Passman at 209 Forsyth Street, New York.

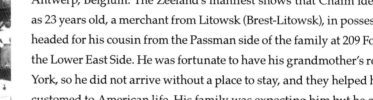

The Lower East Side

By 1900, the University Settlement Society reported that the Tenth Ward on the Lower East Side had a population density greater than the worst sections of Bombay.[77] It was a hurried, energetic neighborhood and some streets were lined with pushcarts and resembled the markets of Russia. Yiddish was spoken and many of the first generation of arrivals never mastered English. But the shtetl didn't have tenements and New York didn't look like home.

The New York tenement was often five stories high and many of the windows opened onto narrow airshafts between the buildings. Indoor toilets were a luxury and most were shared by several families. Almost every family took in boarders and had at least one person sleeping in the kitchen, sometimes on a door that had been removed from its hinges and placed between two chairs. Forsyth Street, where the Passmans lived, was close to one of the centers of prostitution, where the women openly displayed themselves on the stoops of the tenements.[78]

Chaim arrived in winter. He wrote to Yente and ended a letter explaining that his fingers were too cold to continue; heat was a luxury. Chaim was looking to the future. He was excited to tell her he had found a place to learn how to be a cutter in the garment industry. He paid someone to teach him the trade and was unpaid for his long hours as an apprentice. He was happy with the prospect of working for himself as a free person in a free country.[79]

Nearly 60% of employed Jews worked in the garment industry. After the Civil War, there had been a shift from tailor-made to factory-made clothing for men. Toward the beginning of the 1900s, women's wear was also factory made and the center of the industry was New York City. First the Irish and then the Russian Jews filled the jobs of cutters, stitchers, and pressers. Most of these jobs did not require knowledge of English and small workrooms were set up in the tenements as well as in larger factories.

The sweating system began during the Civil War when soldiers' wives and children were employed in making uniforms. It evolved as a method of exploiting labor by supplying materials to workers and paying by the piece for work done in the workers' homes or in small workshops (sweatshops).[80] The employer's home was often also his factory, and work was done in the front room and kitchen, and the family slept in the windowless bedroom. Women could work in their homes and still be able to care for their young children. Tragically, the masses of immigrant workers that made the industry possible also made it possible for their own exploitation. Wages were low and work hours were long and the cramped conditions were unhealthy. Tuberculosis, called the "tailor's disease," was the largest source of deaths among younger adults.[81] Children as young as two years of age could be enlisted in simple tasks such as picking out basting stitches and would have to do this work for hours at a stretch.

Both Benjamin Korman and Solomon Yesersky commented that Chaim was doing "clean work" and Solomon recommended it to his son Samuel. They probably imagined tailoring on a scale they were familiar with in their shtetls. Still,

The east side of Forsyth Street, 2007. This is the side of the street across from the Passman residence. The Passman's block has been torn down and is now the Sara Delano Roosevelt Park and playground. *Photograph by Joan Sohn.*

Photos above: New York tenements. *Library of Congress, Detroit Publishing Company Collection.*

"ABOLISH CH[ILD] SLAVERY!!" in English and Yiddish. This photograph was probably taken during the May 1, 1909 labor parade in New York City. *Library of Congress, George Grantham Bain Collection.*

Hester Street, New York City, 1903. *National Archives and Records Administration.*

there's nothing in his letters that suggests that Chaim was unhappy; in one letter he mentioned that he was offered a business opportunity near his cousins in Newark, New Jersey, but he decided he would be better off finishing his lessons to become a cutter. Employed as a cutter he was never forced to work in the sweatshops.

Not every immigrant was as successful as Chaim and suicide was not infrequent, as it had been in Russia. Chaim was fortunate to have a family to live with and an opportunity to learn a trade. Many of the Jewish immigrants never adapted to America, were unable to earn enough to house and feed their families, and could not give up their shtetl traditions. New York was "the melting pot" and there was pressure to adapt and stop being a "greenhorn." Some of that was pressure to look American, cut the beard, wear store-bought clothing and learn English. Too often, working on Shabbat was a necessity, and the sad irony was that they had left Russia for religious freedom yet had to make religious sacrifices simply to survive. The scholars who had never mastered a trade felt that they had left God behind in Russia.

Delancey Street, 1908. *Photograph by Eugene de Salignac. NYC Municipal Archives.*

The Newspapers

The article, "How Passover Will Be Observed on the East Side" was published in *The New York Times* on April 16, 1905, the date of Chaim's first Passover in America, when he lived on the Lower East Side. The author and illustrator was Bert Levy. The entire article can be read in Appendix A. The illustration shows the pushcarts on the street, a typical sight. *The New York Times* would not have been the newspaper most widely read on the Lower East Side and this article was clearly written for the gentile reader curious about the customs of the new immigrants.

By 1915, when Yiddish journalism peaked, there were five Yiddish language dailies in New York City with a circulation of 500,000 readers. The foremost Yiddish paper that supported both social activism and Americanization was the *Forverts* (*Jewish Daily Forward*), a newspaper that Chaim continued to read to the end of his life. One of the popular features was "A Bintel Brief," Yiddish for "bundle of letters." The editor, Abraham Cahan, wrote advice to the readers who wrote to the *Forward*. Below are two examples:

Dearest friends of the Forward, *I have been jobless for six months now. I have eaten the last shirt on my back and now there is nothing for me but to end my life ...*

Answer: *This is one of the heartrending appeals for help, cries of need that we receive daily. The writer of this letter should go first to the Crisis Conference (address given) and they will not let him starve. And further we ask our readers to let us know if someone can create a job for this unemployed man.*

Dear Editor, Dear Editor, *I am a girl from Galicia (in Poland) and in the shop where I work I sit near a Russian Jew ... (and) he stated that all Galicians were no good ... Why should one worker resent another?*

Answer: *The Galician Jews are just as good and bad as people from other lands. If the Galicians must be ashamed of the foolish and evil ones among them, then the Russians, too, must hide their heads in shame because among them is such an idiot as the acquaintance of our letter writer.*

Independence Hall, 1900. *Library of Congress, Detroit Publishing Company Collection.*

The Liberty Bell was housed for many years inside Independence Hall, as shown in this postcard from the 1950s.

Philadelphia

Philadelphia has always been an "immigrant port and a city of immigrants."[82] It's interesting that many of the people who arrived at the port of Philadelphia moved on to settle elsewhere, while most of the immigrants who settled in Philadelphia arrived at another port, usually New York.[83]

Originally, the Port of Philadelphia, in the early 1900s, was like a smaller Ellis Island. It had the facilities to process waves of immigrants at the terminal on Washington Avenue. It was busy enough that the Pennsylvania Railroad invested in the port and built a line to connect to the immigration terminal so that travelers were able to leave directly for Chicago and other points to the West. There were only two significant impediments to the growth of the port of Philadelphia: the trip was 200 miles longer from Europe to Philadelphia than it was to New York and sometimes the Delaware River froze.[84] As in New York, the first wave of Jewish immigration came from Germany in the 1840s. By the time the huge surge of Jews from Poland and Russia arrived after 1880, the German Jews had adapted and settled into the Philadelphia community. Kathryn Levy Feldman wrote:

> The Eastern European Jews who arrived at the city's port, at the foot of Washington Avenue in South Philadelphia were, for the most part, poor and unskilled. They settled in the alleys and courtyards of Fourth and Fifth Streets, south of Pine, in what would become the equivalent of New York's Lower East Side. They became peddlers, rag men, cigar makers, even "horseradish men" calling out their wares in Yiddish, a dialect that was as foreign to the city's older more established German-Jewish population as it was to their gentile neighbors.[85]

Historian Harry Boonin observed that a fairly sizeable Jewish quarter, mirroring the European shtetls, had sprung up in the areas of old Philadelphia known as Society Hill and Queen Village. He credited this to three primary reasons: rent was cheap, housing was near the sweatshops, and the neighborhood was near the emigrant depot at the foot of Washington Street and the Delaware River. He described it:

> Within this narrowly defined area a new life sprung up. Curbside and pushcart markets were established; teams of horses flying over cobblestone streets made daily runs to the Dock Street wholesale market. Seen on the pavement of the new S. 4th Street pavement market were pickle

Grain wharves of the Pennsylvania Railroad Company on the Delaware River at the foot of Washington Street in 1900. The grain elevator is near the piers of the ocean steamship lines: American, Red Star, and Atlantic Transport. *King's Views of Philadelphia.*

barrels and union enforcers, dreamers and paupers, curbside bookies and curbside elections, saloons, pool halls and feed stores—and in the middle of all this excitement were the synagogues, dozens of them.[86]

Samuel Yesersky added some earthier memories to this picture. His grandson Larry Yerkees was told, "Philadelphia stank in the summer, really stank!" We forget that those horses, "flying" over the cobblestones, left waste wherever they went and there were many, many horses. Fuel exhaust had a very different meaning.

South Philadelphia was our family's neighborhood. Harris Brody, Yente's uncle, lived and worked there, and he was joined by Rose and Samuel Yesersky and also by their cousin Bessie Priluker, in 1902. Louis arrived in 1903, Yente in 1905, and Lazar in 1906. Jacob Smigelski also arrived in 1906 and his wife, Gittle (Harris Brody and Miriam Yesersky's sister) followed with their children in 1907. Solomon and Miriam brought the younger Yesersky children in 1907. The 1910 Federal Census shows that Isaac, Louis, Lazar, Celia, and William lived together at 336 S. 3rd Street.

The photograph on the left is the Dock Street Wholesale Market, about 1908. On the right, is the foot of Market Street, between 1900 and 1910. The words, "Bassett's Ice Cream," are on the delivery wagon at the right. *Library of Congress, Detroit Publishing Company Collection.*

Philadelphia didn't have the dense tenement housing of New York. Most of the residential buildings the immigrants lived in were in the old part of the city near the docks; these were smaller attached houses that were shared by multiple families. The 1900 U.S. Federal Census shows two other families living at 418 Fitzwater Street along with Harris Brody and his children. Philadelphia also didn't have the industries, like Pittsburgh's steel mills, which attracted many unskilled laborers. The more skilled workers in Philadelphia were paid higher wages and many people were able to buy their own homes; "several hundred thousand row houses were built between 1880 and 1920 and by the twenties almost half of all Philadelphians owned their own homes and the city's population density was remarkably low."[87]

No. 1 K 5 6 6 5 This beautiful massive Morris Chair is made of thoroughly seasoned and specially selected quarter sawed oak, highly polished and finished in a rich golden color. Note the massive carvings on the wide curved arms; heavy claw feet and curved front rail. Cushions are reversible and made of best quality of verona, crushed plush, fabricold (imitation leather) and genuine leather, filled with hair and deeply tufted. Back is adjustable to several comfortable positions by our patent rod and ratchet attachment. Beauty of design is combined with solid construction, making this chair the most desirable piece we have ever offered. Shipped direct from our factory near Chicago or Central New York. Shipping weight, 75 pounds.

$9.75

Verona	Crushed Plush	Fabricold	Gen. Leather
Price ...$9.75	$11.25	$11.55	$16.95

Above: Yetta and Hyman's Morris Chair may have been one of their earliest pieces of furniture, and is very similar to the chair shown in the 1908 Sears Roebuck catalog. It was always in the farmhouse kitchen, and any ill child was placed in the chair to stay warm near the stove. It was one of the few pieces from the farm that Hyman kept after Yetta died. Now it is in the home of James Korman, Hyman's great grandson.

Right: State of Pennsylvania Marriage License application, Hyman Korman and Jette Jeziersky. It shows they reside at the same address, which is probably Harris Brody's home. It is most likely that Hyman actually continued to reside in New York until the September wedding. Hyman's occupation was not caterer; the clerk must have misunderstood Hyman's heavy accent when he said "cutter."

Hyman's awkward signature shows that he is not yet comfortable with English.

Chaim left his new life in New York to come to Philadelphia to marry Yente. They applied for a marriage license on August 3, 1905, and the application shows that they both lived at 230 Greenwich Street, which was most likely one of Harris Brody's South Philadelphia properties, as Harris received mail at the same address that September. Soon afterward, an envelope addressed to Mr. Korman at 323 S.3rd Street was postmarked October 24, 1905; perhaps the newlyweds found their own apartment.

Like New York, Philadelphia was also a center of the American garment industry and Chaim resumed his work as a cutter. (The clerk who filled out their marriage license application must have misunderstood his accent because the form lists "caterer" as his occupation!) The Kormans stayed in South Philadelphia for a while, but Russian Jews and new immigrants were also moving into the homes in the area north of Vine Street known as the Northern Liberties, which was becoming the center of the garment trades.

"Progress" was an important idea to Americans as was America's reputation as the land of "opportunity." The successful Centennial Exhibition World's Fair in 1876 showcased American invention and ingenuity and the Europeans got a look at the United States as a nation that rivaled, and even surpassed, Europe. America wasn't simply a country of farmers.

Our family came to a city that was alive with new construction in anticipation of a booming future. The Reading Terminal train station opened at 12th and Market Streets in 1893, eight years after the Pennsylvania Railroad opened its Broad Street Station at 15th and Market. The Broad Street Station was torn down in 1953, but the Reading Terminal remains, although it is now part of the Penn-

The Centennial Exhibition of 1876

The Centennial Exhibition of 1876, the first official World's Fair in the United States, was held in Philadelphia to celebrate the 100th anniversary of the signing of the Declaration of Independence in Philadelphia. The Centennial ushered in an unprecedented era of invention as America moved from the age of steam to the age of electricity and the internal combustion engine.[84] It was officially the International Exhibition of Arts, Manufactures, and Products of the Soil and Mine, and it showcased many of the latest inventions such as Alexander Graham Bell's first telephone, Remington's typewriter, Heinz Ketchup, Hires Root Beer, and the Wallace-Farmer Electric Dynamo, a precursor to electric light. The right arm and torch of the Statue of Liberty were presented at the Exhibition and, for a fee of 50 cents, visitors could climb the ladder to the balcony; money raised this way was used to fund the rest of the statue.

This was truly a World's Fair, with participation from 37 countries, 11 of them contributing buildings. The Centennial served to bring Americans into contact with foreigners as never before.[85]

In all, there were more than 200 buildings constructed within the Fair grounds, which were surrounded by a fence nearly three miles long. Most of the original buildings were designed to be temporary structures, but Memorial Hall and Horticultural Hall were constructed to be permanent. Horticultural Hall was badly damaged by Hurricane Hazel in 1954 and then demolished, but Memorial Hall became the original home for the Philadelphia Art Museum[86] and currently houses the Please Touch Museum for children.

Despite a severe heat wave that summer, from May to November there were more than 10 million admissions to the Fair, some of which were multiple visits.

Memorial Hall, Fairmount Park, 1876 (lithograph). *Library of Congress.*

Pennsylvania Railroad's Broad Street Station at 15th and Market Streets, 1900. *King's Views of Philadelphia.*

The Reading Terminal at 12th and Market Streets, 1900. *King's Views of Philadelphia.*

Chestnut Street looking west from Ninth Street, 1900. *King's Views of Philadelphia.*

City Hall and William Penn Statue (inset), 1900. Note the people standing at the base of the sculpture when it was displayed in the courtyard of the building prior to its installation atop the clock tower. *King's Views of Philadelphia.*

sylvania Convention Center. The Terminal was built on the site of an open air market that had been in use since 1653; the market was relocated a block north and the train station was built above it. The Terminal had a modern and daring design and at the time, the train shed was one of the largest single-span arched roof structures in the world. It is now the world's oldest such structure, and the only one left in the United States.

City Hall, at Broad and Market Streets, had been completed by 1901, fulfilling William Penn's vision for a public building in the center of his five planned squares. It remains the largest municipal building in North America and perhaps the world and its exterior remains relatively unchanged from its original design. Alexander Milne Calder's 37-foot-tall statue of William Penn on the top of the clock tower is still the tallest sculpture on the top of any building in the world.[88]

Moses King published a successful series of illustrated travel guides to major American cities. His 1900 monograph on Philadelphia described Chestnut Street between Ninth and Broad: "This row, beginning with the Federal Building, containing the Post Office, U.S. Courts, etc., and including the structures occupied by the 'Philadelphia Record,' Penn Mutual Life Insurance Company and City Trust Company, is one of the chief architectural features of the city, and

travelers say is not surpassed by any similar business stretch anywhere."[89] Fannye Yesersky Taylor recalls that her mother Bessie Yesersky told her that she and Yetta would walk from South Philadelphia to Chestnut Street to make deposits into "the bank." These imposing structures, whose banking halls were lined with marble and designed to be awe-inspiring, like cathedrals, assured depositors that nothing could go wrong with their savings.

It's easy to imagine that Yetta and Bessie stopped for a snack at the new Automat that Joe Horn and Frank Hardart opened at 818 Chestnut Street in 1902. Horn and Hardart's restaurants certainly became a family favorite in later years. But aside from the novelty of the food service and its high quality, the Automat was another sign that a small businessman could, with some creativity, succeed in the Philadelphia marketplace.

Convenient public transit was an important component of city life in a way that is unfamiliar to most of us. There were very few private automobiles, but there was a trolley line on almost every downtown street. Many people never learned to drive because there was simply no need. The last horse-drawn car ceased operation in 1897 and the first electric trolley was introduced on Catharine and Bainbridge Streets in 1892. By 1902, many independent companies had merged to form the Philadelphia Rapid Transit Company. Trolley usage peaked in 1911 when close to 4000 cars operated over 86 routes. In 2008, SEPTA ran 87 routes and 2664 vehicles in all of Philadelphia. [90]

Market Street, between Broad Street and the Delaware River, was the location for many of the city's great department stores. In 1876 John Wanamaker built a large store that he gradually replaced to become the majestic building he opened in 1911, across from City Hall.[91] Inspired by Galleries Lafayette in Paris, Wa-

Horn & Hardart's original Automat at 818 Chestnut Street.
The original automatic food dispensers were designed in Switzerland, manufactured in Germany, and sent to Philadelphia by ship. Later systems were made in America for the local market. A customer could deposit a nickel and open a door to remove a food selection. A combination of quality, low prices, and novelty made the restaurants successful, and generations of Philadelphians and New Yorkers have fond memories of the Automat.

Sarah Moss explained that Mom was a diabetic. They would travel downtown for Mom's check-up and blood sugar monitoring with Mom's doctor and then go directly to the Automat for an afternoon dessert treat.

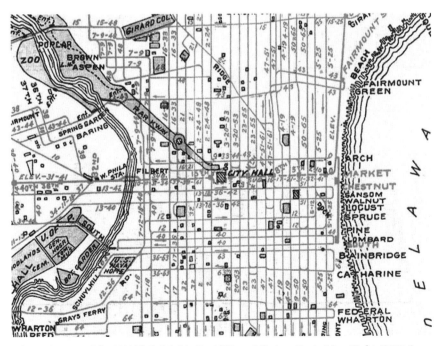

Above: Section of the 1923 Philadelphia Rapid Transit System Route Map. Right: PRT tokens.

The trolley on Market Street in front of Gimbel Brothers Department Store. *Print & Picture Collection, Free Library of Philadelphia.*

namaker's had nine floors for shopping, circling a dramatic central atrium, and the levels were accessed by newly-developed electric elevators.[92] The Lit Brothers opened their first store in 1893 at Eighth and Market Streets, and by the time they opened their flagship store in 1907, it filled an entire block bounded by Seventh, Eighth, Market, and Arch Streets.[93] Snellenburg's department store moved from South Street, where it was founded in 1869, to 12th and Market Streets, in 1889.[94] Blum Brothers (which later became the Blum Store on Chestnut Street), was at Tenth and Market; Gimbel Brothers was at Ninth and Market; and Strawbridge and Clothier was at Eighth and Market.

These stores were like palaces. The storefronts showed merchandise in large window displays along the sidewalks, and the store interiors were grand, with soaring ceilings and fabulous decorations. The shopping experience was nothing like it was in the familiar general stores in immigrant neighborhoods. In the department stores customers could see small items in glass display cases and walk among racks of clothing. John Wanamaker purchased the largest pipe organ in the world and installed it on the balcony above his store's Grand Court. A large, bronze sculpture of an eagle in the Grand Court became the meeting spot for generations of Philadelphians. Historian Daniel Boorstin noted, "The atmosphere made shoppers feel special, offering distractions from ordinary life intended to encourage impulse buying. Department stores further removed themselves from ordinary life by providing various cultural events throughout the day, including organ music, fashion shows, and lectures. Some also offered babysitting."[95] Each store had its own elegant restaurant dining room. I don't think that there was anything like these stores anywhere near our families' Russian homes, and the immigrants must have been dazzled.

In these stores, the public, including the recent immigrants from Eastern European shtetls, also learned how to be modern consumers. The department stores taught their customers a sense of style and instilled a desire for beauty in their daily lives. The merchandising was a course in adaptation to the new American way. While they probably shopped locally in the "mom and pop" general stores in South Philadelphia, in a Yiddish-speaking environment that could provide all their needs, the lure of Market Street was undeniable.

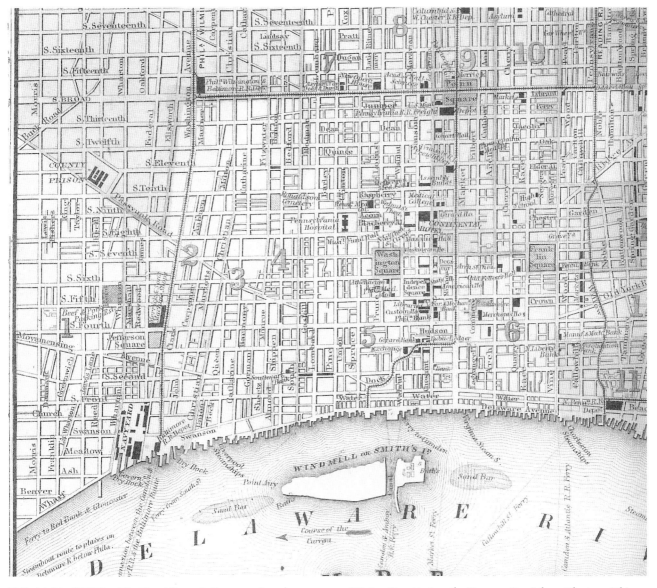

Philadelphia, 1867. Franklin Street (lower left corner of map) was renamed Tasker Street before the Kormans lived there. The top of this map faces west.

Rabbi Benjamin Korinman

Title page, *Chelkat Binyomin*, The Portion of Benjamin, written by Rabbi Benjamin Korinman.

Rabbi Benjamin and Hudel Korinman, Yechezkel and Chaya Korinman

Benjamin Korinman is the bearded man in the single surviving photograph (shown above), and the family always speaks of him with great respect and awe. In his honor, we are a family of "Benjamins." For most of his descendants, he's the mysterious rabbi who wrote a book that we don't understand because we are not scholarly enough to grasp the meaning.

We wonder what to call him. Sometimes his family name is written Korinman, and at other times it is Korman. His father's Russian name was Mordko (Mordecai Tsevi in Hebrew) and he had at least two brothers, Velvyl and Yoyl, and a sister, Leah. Benjamin and his wife Hudel had two sons, Yechezkel (Oscar) Korinman, in 1877, and Chaim (Hyman) Korman in 1881.

Velvyl Korman's daughter Leah Deganith wrote this tribute to her uncle Rabbi Korman that is included in the "Judges and Torah Sages" section of the Brest-Litovsk entry of *The Encyclopedia of the Jewish Diaspora:*

I think that not many of the Brest residents knew this particular person, who for decades bent over his scrunched up pieces of paper and wrote his treatise on the interpretation of the Sabbath. I remember his figure from my childhood, and his glowing face, dreamy eyes, and soft hands that stroked my head.

I was rarely privileged to be in his presence—in my home he was spoken of with the greatest respect. When my father would mention Reb Benjamin's name, his face would light up. For thirty years, his older brother Benjamin wrote his book *Helkat Benjamin* (Benjamin's Portion), a commentary on the Sabbath. Where did the title come from? He said, "this is my entire portion of the world's effort."

For thirty years he did not look at the outside world. He had a wife and children, but they were outside the realm of his vision. My father and his brothers financially supported his household. My father was an expert in the construction of railway tracks—he wandered with his family all over Greater Russia—the steppes and remote settlements. He would set up temporary buildings and houses for the specialist workers, such as the engineers, tradesmen and the priest—and one Jewish family.

My grandfather would tell me about Brest with tears in his eyes, about the synagogue of Israel Wolf, the city parks, the King's Garden. According to his description, it seemed to me that it was the most beautiful park in the world.

Arriving in Brest after W.W.I, I found a neglected garden and Israel Wolf's synagogue was no more than a wooden shack. I understood that in grandfather's eyes, longing for his hometown, they seemed thus.

My father, who had always lived amongst gentiles, considered his brother Benjamin as the light of his life. On one of his visits to Brest, he built a synagogue in the vicinity of my uncle's home, so that he could sit and study in peace and be immersed in the Torah.

My uncle would not accept the position of rabbi, as he did not want to make a living from the Torah. His whole life was dedicated to writing this book, for which he had received permission from Rabbi Chaim Soloveitchik. When he finished the book, my father traveled for three days from Orenburg to Brest for the celebration. He helped edit the book and prepare it for publication.

Once, after much pleading, my uncle agreed to see the emissaries who had come to see him about becoming the Rabbi of their shtetl. By the way, they requested to see his wife, the Rebbetzen, who was short and no beauty. She did not find favor with the emissaries, who did not take kindly to her. My uncle told my father of this event with great amazement: "Did you know that the Rebbetzen is not good looking?" He himself did not know of this his whole life.

Leah Deganith's recollection was written almost 40 years after the Rabbi's death. I think she wrote with great affection and admiration, but I can't accept

Velvyl Korinman and his wife.

Leah Deganith, 1930s, in the theater production of Doom.

Leah Deganith was born in 1904, in Brest and passed away in 1985, in Israel. She initially attained fame as a leading actress at the Habima and Ohel Theaters. She married Moshe Halevy, the theater's founder. In addition to being a successful actress, she wrote and recorded songs, including some that are considered classics of the Israeli repertoire. The Ohel Theater closed in 1969, after which Leah turned to painting. She studied painting in Paris and Tel Aviv and exhibited in Israel and abroad.

Rabbi Chaim Soloveitchik, 1853–1918, founder of the Brisker approach to study.

Rabbi Isaac Elchanan Spector, 1817–1896, Benjamin Korinman's teacher in Kovno.

Various institutions are named after Rabbi Spector, including the Rabbi Isaac Elchanan Theological Seminary (RIETS), part of Yeshiva University in New York. His first wife, Sara Raizel Yesersky, the daughter of Reb Eliezer Yesersky, and his wife, Bluma, was from Volkovisk and was part of Solomon Yesersky's family.

her notion that his children went unnoticed. I have read his letters to his son Chaim and they are warm, loving, and full of news about family and concern for his children.

Goldie Seiderman shared stories she had been told about Rabbi Korinman, her great grandfather. Her grandmother, Benjamin's daughter-in-law Chaya (Ida Korman), told her he was a progressive, forward-thinking Rabbi and advised her on child rearing. He told her she should not scold a child in public, and humiliate; she was to address the problem in private. He was also kind and helpful to her when she went into a depression after a second death of one of her children. He encouraged her and counseled her that she had mourned enough and that she had four other children who needed her.

Oscar left for Philadelphia in 1913 and expected to bring his family soon after, but the outbreak of WWI and then the Russian Revolution of 1917 stranded them in Russia. Goldie's mother, Anna, was seventeen when she and her family left Brisk for Philadelphia in 1921. She remembered living near her grandparents' home and enjoyed seeing them often. Goldie said that Anna "adored" Benjamin and, in Oscar's absence, Benjamin was her surrogate father. She said that he didn't seem to be as Old-World traditional as some of the Rabbis, and she described him as "modern Orthodox." He said that the children were the most important thing and that they were welcome anytime, even if he was studying Torah.

Anna also remembered his generosity; she said he often invited "strays" for Shabbat, a habit which displeased his wife. It's possible that she was managing the family finances and feeding another hungry person put a strain on her resources for the week.

Anna also remembered Rabbi Chaim Soloveitchik, the famous Brisker Rabbi, nodding to her grandfather in respect. Rabbi Soloveitchik had developed a new

Hudel Korinman, cabinet card front and back, photographed in Brest. The pencil-written address, 628 Tasker Street, is Chaim and Yente's Philadelphia home.

analytical method of studying the Talmud and his yeshiva was famous throughout Eastern Europe. His method was different from the Hasidic method, which was much more emotional. He had encouraged Rabbi Benjamin to write his book and wrote a personal commendation that was included when it was published. This commendation from Rabbi Soloveitchik is still recognized as an indication that Chelkat Binyomin is an important work.

The following biography—probably written by Rabbi Pinchos J. Chazin of Temple Sholom with information provided by Hyman Korman—was part of the program book for the dedication of the Rabbi Benjamin Korman Memorial Chapel at Temple Sholom in Philadelphia, on November 16, 1952:

Polish passport for Izzy, Max, and Sam Korman, used to travel to America in 1921.

> Rabbi Benjamin Korman was born in the year 1857, in Brisk, Lithuania, son of Mordecai and Sarah Passman Korman. From his early youth he devoted himself assiduously to the study of the Talmud.
>
> He was a disciple of one of the great Talmudic scholars of his day, the revered Rabbi Isaac Elchanan Spector, from whom he received his rabbinic ordination at the Yeshiva of Kovno. To this center of learning he came as a student and remained as a teacher.
>
> He married Hudel Marzovitz, a pious woman descended from a lineage of scholars and rabbis. They had two children, Oscar since deceased, and Hyman, who came to America shortly after the turn of the century.
>
> Rabbi Korman early felt the need for an up-to-date commentary on the Talmudic Tractate Shabbat, to include the ancient codifiers and also the more recent commentators. For many years he devoted himself to this labor of love, finally publishing a very substantial volume to a projected two-volume comprehensive work in 1913 entitled PORTION OF BENJAMIN. This significant volume bears a forward by the Chief Rabbi of Grodno, Lithuania, Rabbi Chaim Soloveitchik.
>
> In 1919, Benjamin Korman, man of piety and learning, lifetime student of the Talmud departed this earth. "May the memory of the righteous be for a blessing."

Anna Korman and her father Yechezkel.

Chaya and Yechezkel Korinman.

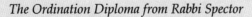

The Ordination Diploma from Rabbi Spector

Verily, these words of truth may be ascribed to that worthy man, the rabbi ... , a native of ... , with whom I have discussed fully, and [found] he is filled with the Word of the Lord in Talmud and in the Codes. He is also an excellent preacher, preaching what is moral and practicing the morals he preaches. Therefore I say: Let his power and might in the Torah be encouraged. Let him teach and decide in matters of monetary law; dietary and rituals; get and halizah rites; laws relating to pure and impure. And may it be the will of the Merciful to secure him an honorable position according to his honor. As the said rabbi deserves and is able to lead a holy community [lit. "sheep"], I have signed this week-day, ... , day in month, ... , and year...

So says Isaac Elhanan, who dwells with the holy congregation of Kovno.

Hyman Korman/ Chaim
Yetta Yesersky Korman/ Yente
Solomon and Miriam Yesersky

Although he was raised in the home of Rabbi Benjamin Korman, respected teacher and scholar, Chaim Korman chose to pursue a life in business. His uncles, Yoyl and Velvyl Korman, were successful railway builders in Russia and Chaim joined them in their work. Chaim's grandson Leonard Korman wrote a school paper, near the time of his bar mitzvah, about his ancestors and explained:

> This occupation made it necessary for him to be away from home most of his early manhood, as these railroads stretched through many miles of wilderness in the undeveloped regions of Russia. The only time they came to town was on holidays, at which time they left their barracks on the road and spent the holidays with friendly families, who were good enough to act as substitutes for their immediate relatives who were many miles away.

> It was on one such occasion, in 1903, that my grandfather met my grandmother who was the daughter of a very wealthy family in this particular town where they chose to spend their period of leave for the purpose of celebrating a traditional Jewish holiday. My grandmother's parents operated stage coach lines from one state to another, carrying passengers and mail for the government of Russia.

The Yeserskys lived in Svisloch, and their lives were about to change. The new railway was being constructed through their shtetl and it would be completed in 1906, making their stagecoach and mail transportation business obsolete, and two of their 10 children had already moved to Philadelphia. But in the winter of 1903 they housed Chaim, a handsome young man who was away from his home at Passover. Leonard continued:

> My grandmother used to relate to me how my grandfather first took her ice skating on the town lake, and how her steady beau skirted the lake on skates with jealousy because of this new rival who had come to town. It was this rivalry for the hand of grandmother that probably prompted my grandfather to leave his country and occupation, and bring my grandmother with him to America to seek new opportunities.

It really is a romantic story. Perhaps it's not quite as uncomplicated as Leonard imagined, but that doesn't diminish the romance. Leonard may not have known about Chaim's military service and that it was a huge issue; Chaim's letters make it clear that he wanted to be free of both the army and the Czar.

Chaim met Yente in Svisloch when she was 20 and he was 22. Railroad building is slow work and they must have had time to get to know each other—and the former steady beau didn't stand a chance. It's evident from the letters that he also became friendly with her family and siblings, some of whom were his contemporaries and some who were young children. He knew her Aunt Chaya and her girlfriends.

Berton Korman remembers that Pop described some of his work for the railroad. The housing for the workers was built of logs cut like the familiar "Lincoln Logs" toy. These buildings would be situated so that the workers did not have to travel more than half a day to the section of track they were building. As the railroad progressed, the housing would be disassembled and moved. The building inspectors were anti-Semite Russians who came to see the log cabins. They usually found fault with the bottom log so that the whole building had to be disassembled and rebuilt. Eventually Pop learned to cut a "chip" in the bottom log, wait for it to be discovered, replace the chip, and have the building approved when the inspector returned.

Yente's father, Solomon, was also a scholar and descended from a prestigious line of Rabbis. He was the great grandson of Rabbi Yehuda Leib Halevi who had emigrated from Frankfurt am Main, Germany to Wolkovisk (where Solomon was born, about 18 miles from Svisloch) about 1760–1770. Miriam, Solomon's wife, supported his scholarship and ran both the stagecoach line and the home. She was a petite, wiry woman and her family respected her authority. Her grandchildren called her "Little Bubbe."[97]

The Yesersky home was a busy, lively place. Willie (Velvyle) was five years old and the youngest. Yente said that they all sat around one large table at mealtime, and there might be the 12 family members and some boarders from the coach line. Miriam sometimes hired a helper but Yente undoubtedly assisted her mother with the cooking and the younger children.[98] Yente was educated as girls were generally educated at the time; she could write letters in Yiddish, but her writing was not as grammatically or stylistically elegant as the men's. Her daughter Sarah later said that Yente was never a "reader."

Food was traditional, Russian, and Jewish. The Yeserskys maintained a religious home and kept kosher. Recipes were handed down, and when I asked my mother how to prepare the foods her mother cooked, she said that there were no written records. "She cooked by the handful, adding a *bissel* of this and that." Yente became a good cook and is remembered for her barley soup, tongue, and large pans of petcha. She made farmer's cheese, hanging the soured milk in a cloth bag and added lung to her liver knishes to make them light. She cooked gefilte fish in a cauldron and put a piece of fish skin on each ball to make it look pretty. Canning vegetables and making vegetable soup was a summer ritual.[99]

The first of the family letters we have is written from Chaim to Yente in July of 1904, and it's evident that they had corresponded for some time, although he still addressed her using the formal form ("ir") and not the familiar form ("du"), which he used in his later letters.[100] At this point, Chaim had been in the army for about a year, stationed in Smolensk, and was anticipating another three years of service. Russia had been fighting the Russo-Japanese War for five months, and he wrote that his regiment was "for the moment not set to go to the east. We are set to go as it will be needed."[101] He wanted Yente to wait for him but understood that he was in no position to make promises to her and he explained:

> But you are taking a very difficult thing on yourself. You have to quarrel with your parents this way for a time and you cannot yet go around to anybody, and holding it to yourself in your heart is very difficult, and, as I understand, you are too soft in this regard. About this I think about how to make it easier for you, but unfortunately I have no means for this.[102]

At some point in the next months following this letter to Yente, he decided it was the time to leave the army and Russia. He made plans to go to New York, and he asked her to marry him in America. Her parents knew and were pleased.

The other person who should have been told was Rabbi Korman. There was romance in Russia, but there were rules for everything, including romance. Rabbi

Berton Korman remembers that his great-grandmother Miriam sometimes came to visit them near Newmarket, PA where the Kormans farmed during WW II. Mom ran the household, which included Pop, their children Max, Sam, and Sarah, their daughters-in-law, four grandchildren, and a maid. Mom was always a strong force; the entire family income was delivered to her and she dispensed funds as needed. She was not particularly interested in gardening and outdoor activities but the home was her domain. Bert recalls that when Little Bubbe arrived, there was a noticeable power shift and Yetta "trembled" in her own kitchen. I like to think of Miriam as the "Alpha Mom!"

The 1907 immigration documents show that arriving in New York, Solomon was 54 years old and 5′ 3″ tall. Miriam was age 51 and just 5 feet tall. Both were described as fair, with brown hair and eyes. Miriam may have become even more petite as she aged, which lead to her name "Little Bubbe."

Clifton House, built in 1801 on Bethlehem Pike in Whitemarsh Township, PA, was once the Sandy Run Tavern. It is now the Fort Washington Historical Society headquarters. The 1930, U.S. Federal Census shows that Solomon and Miriam Yesersky owned the property. They operated it as an inn, a destination for summer farm holidays.

Korman was clear to his son when he wrote:

> And concerning the match in Sislovitz [the Yiddish name for Svisloch] … in this you have gone beyond the limits of ethics and respect in that you kept this matter from me when you were here, for then I would have gone with you to Sislovitz, and it would have been done in a more pleasant way. You have acted foolishly. Nevertheless, I forgive you and I hold no grudge against you for childishness took hold of you and you imagined that I would prevent it. Therefore you were afraid to tell me. This is not the case, but, on the contrary I would have strengthened your hand in the matter in the best way possible …[103]

Chaim's uncles, still building the railroad in the Svisloch area, traveled to meet the Yesersky family and found them to be extremely suitable. They would have been impressed with Solomon's lineage and his personal scholarship, as well as his ability to provide Yente with a dowry. Yente traveled to Brisk to meet the Kormans and they were very pleased. An official engagement contract was negotiated between the two families. The romance was back on track.

The Stagecoaches and Mail

Say "stagecoach" to most twenty-first century people and the image that comes immediately to mind is the Western "shoot em up" film. Then, because American history is so abbreviated, Americans tend to think that whatever transportation that was in existence a hundred and fifty years ago, is antique in nature, stretching back into the mists of time. The fact is that the closed passenger wagon drawn by multiple horses is an innovation of the late eighteenth century. It had a heyday of around eighty years. Its start was the development of good postal roads and of governments willing to pay for conveyance of the post. Its end was foreshadowed by the development of a road that could take thousands of pounds of load as well as the mails – the railway. But even after the railroads entered our part of the then Russian Empire in the 1870s, the stagecoaches held on. Conveyances that could go where the railroad lines did not were of great value for several more decades.

This is an excerpt from "Stagecoaches and the Mail in the Geography of Lyakhovichi" by Deborah G. Glassman, copyright 2004.
www.shtetlinks.jewishgen.org/lyakhovichi
More of this article can be found in Appendix B on page 109.

My mother's first language, in Philadelphia, was Yiddish, and she did not really speak English until she started school. Hyman and Yetta spoke Yiddish at home, but when they didn't want the children to understand a conversation, they switched to Russian.

The name Yente is derived from the Old Italian, gentile, meaning amiable or high-born. Over the years this lovely name became synonymous with a gossipy, meddling woman. Perhaps Sholem Aleichem is to blame; he chose Yenta as the name for the village matchmaker in his stories about Tevye the milkman. A Yente wasn't always a yenta!

Rose Yesersky and Harris Brody

My mother always told me that her Aunt Rose was the most beautiful of the Yesersky daughters. Rose was so beautiful that her uncle, Harris Brody, a man 24 years older than she, approached his sister Miriam and her husband, Solomon, in Svisloch and asked for permission to marry their daughter Rochel. Harris Brody had lived in Philadelphia for some time and had a thriving stable and livery business in South Philadelphia.[104] His business at 233 Tasker Street was not far from the docks where the steamships brought immigrants from Liverpool, and many of those people needed to rent a horse and wagon to deliver their baggage to their new homes.[105] He may have been a widower with two children, but Solomon and Miriam agreed to the marriage and allowed Rose to go to Philadelphia.

Harris Brody's letterhead in 1905 showing his stables at 233–235 Tasker Street and his residence at 230 Greenwich Street. Street maps show that the two properties met at the rear of each.

Harris Brody had arrived in America in 1882,[106] and I think he was the first of our family in Philadelphia. If he had decided to settle elsewhere, we would not be a Philadelphia family! His business had evolved from selling hay to renting horses. He was a wealthy man in June, 1902, when 17-year-old Rose Yesersky arrived from Svisloch to marry him.[107] For a time, they continued to live in his home at 416 Fitzwater Street, not far from both his business and the Washington Avenue Immigration Terminal.[108]

Harris Brody was both wealthy and generous. His granddaughter Beverly Pomerantz remembers stories about his business dealings and that she was told that he used a handshake to seal a deal, and, surprisingly, he never learned to read English. He asked his daughter Sara to make his bank deposits, sometimes as much as $10,000 in cash, a very sizeable sum at the time. In 1919, he purchased a 300-acre farm on Dolington Road in Newtown Township, Bucks County, and lived there with his family until 1926. Fannye Yesersky Taylor, Rose's niece, recalls that he raised racehorses; later the stone farmhouse became a popular restaurant called Lavender Hall. He also owned property in New Jersey and was involved in the excavation work at the new Fort Dix.

Harris was the man who made it possible for the entire Yesersky family to come to Philadelphia; over and over his name is mentioned in their immigration documents.

Bessie Priluker, Rose's cousin, arrived in Philadelphia in September 1902 and Harris met her at the dock. Bessie moved into the Brody home and they allowed

Photos of siblings, from the top: Miriam Brody Yesersky with her daughter Rose, 1942; Harris Brody, 1931; and Gittle Brody (Smigelski) Samuels with granddaughter Janis, 1944.

An enameled coffee pot and mug, blue with white speckles.

her to stay for a year so that she could attend school and learn English. Yente arrived at Ellis Island on July 18, 1905 and immediately joined her sister Rose's household in Philadelphia. Her immigration papers show that she was going to her Uncle Harris Brody on Castor Road, Frankford, where he had a feed store and horses. This may be the place where the Brodys hosted Chaim and Yente's wedding. The following March, Rose's brother Lazar landed in New York and his papers indicated that he was travelling to his Uncle Harris Brody's at Frankford Street. Immigration papers are often slightly incorrect and Lazar was probably headed for the Castor Road address in Frankford.

Chaim left his new life in New York to come to Philadelphia to marry Yente. They applied for a marriage license on August 3, 1905, and the application shows that they both lived at 230 Greenwich Street, which was most likely one of Harris Brody's South Philadelphia properties, as Harris received mail at the same address that September. Soon afterward, an envelope was sent to Mr. Korman at 323 S. 3rd Street, postmarked October 24, 1905; perhaps the newlyweds found their own apartment.

Rose was already a married woman in Philadelphia when her older sister Yente met Chaim Korman. She certainly knew about him from Yente's letters and she most likely was very curious and eager to meet him. She was also Yente's expert advisor on all things American and had no trouble offering sage advice. Yente was eager to prepare herself with the things she would need for her new life and she was happy to rely on Rose's new knowledge. I wonder how much experience Rose drew upon when she told Yente, "Copper is not so much in style because it is absolutely not necessary in America. For 50 cents (kopeks) you can get the biggest and nicest pot. Here pots are blue and white."[109] I think she was telling her sister that she should leave the good copper pots behind in favor of blue enameled pots that were really only good for boiling water!

Fannye Taylor also remembers Aunt Rose's beauty as well as her enthusiasm and grace as a hostess. Fannye says that Rose always wanted the family to visit, and as soon as you walked in the door, Rose urged you to sit down and eat. One of Rose's requests was that Yente bring her a larger samovar from Russia so that she could serve larger quantities of hot tea.[110]

As stipulated in Chaim and Yente's engagement contract, their wedding was celebrated at Rose and Harris's home in Frankford. They had a place near Cottman Street and Hartshorne Lane,[111] which is now known as Castor Avenue.[112] My mother also told me that the wedding was fabulous and lasted three days, which was the custom in Svisloch.[113]

The Grodno Yeserskys

The photograph at the left is of a gathering of the Yesersky family of Grodno at the 1910 funeral of Hirsh Yesersky, Solomon's brother. Feige, his widow, is in the center of the picture.

Hirsh's son Louis Isard settled in Philadelphia and wrote this short family history. A portion of the hand-written original appears on the left:

About 1760 to 1770 Rabbi Jehuda (author of the book "Hafikei Jehuda") emigrated from Frankford am Main, Germany to Wolkovisk or Slonim (State of Grodno Russian Poland) to become a local Rabbi. His grandson Samuel who was my paternal grandfather and also my father Hirsh-Zevi, were both born in Wolkovisk (State of Grodno.) My grandfather Samuel was in liquor distilling business, died in Wolkovisk. My father after being married settled in Grodno and was also engaged in the distillery business.

I was born in Grodno Aug 16th, 1880 and was named Lieber after my father's maternal grandfather who was a rabbi in the city of Slonim (State of Grodno) and who's [sic] son was Itzhock Elchanan who first became Rabbi in town of Slonim and eventually famous Rabbi of Kovno. My paternal grandmother was his sister.

Louis Isard

My father's brother who arrived in U.S. when the New York elevated was built and whos [sic] name was Leib Yesersky was one of the founders of Yeshiva of Itzhock Elchanan in New York City.

Unfortunately, Louis Isard has presented some historical inconsistencies concerning Rabbi Itzhock Elchanan. He is most likely a relation, but not in the exact way Louis explained it. Rabbi Jehuda was most likely Rabbi Yehuda Low Halevi Edel of Slonim and his son was Joseph Eliezer Lieber Edel. Yeshiva University has lost all of the early records from its founding as the Yeshiva of Itzhock Elchanan, so Lieb Yesersky's story cannot be verified.

49

The Jewish Colonial Trust

The Jewish Colonial Trust was the "financial instrument of the Zionist movement." It was founded by Theodor Herzl in 1899 to hold the money of the Zionists in trust and, at the same time, to act as a bank and carry on business in the commercial world. It became the parent company of the Anglo- Palestine Bank, the predecessor of Bank Leumi (The National Bank of Israel).

The company's activities in the diplomatic field focused on the purchase of the right of settlement in the Land of Israel from the Ottoman government. In the financial field, it granted credit for the establishment of Zionist activities in the Land of Israel.

Early in the 20th century, the company offered about 250,000 shares at par value of £ 1. The information on the stock certificate was written in English and Hebrew on the face and on the back was translated into German, Russian, and French. The illustrations show a scene of prayer at the Western Wall in Jerusalem, a farmer planting seed, a metal-working factory, and crates being unloaded at a dock.

Most shares were sold as £1 notes and many were purchased in installments. Some of these £1 shares were purchased jointly by groups of as many as eight people.

Solomon Yesersky supported the Zionists by purchasing one share, No. 52359, in Swislotz, Russia on March 15, 1901. The original certificate was found with the letters in Hyman Korman's apartment. Only one of the six dividend warrants (coupons) is missing and was probably cashed in Russia.

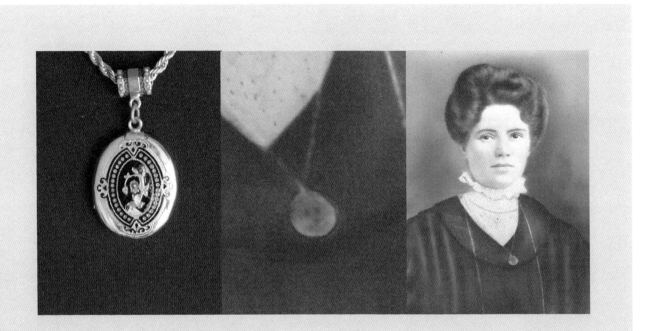

The Locket

This is the locket that has been passed down to the eldest daughter in each generation of my family. I know it came from Miriam Brody Yesersky to Yetta Yesersky Korman, to Sarah Korman Moss and to me, Joan Moss Sohn. I think it is the locket in Yetta's portrait, shown above. The photograph was "touched-up" at the time it was first printed, so I squint and compare, and I really think it's the one. According to the story, she should not have had it yet but her mother may have given it to her as she left for America. There was always the terrible possibility that they would never be together again.

My mother told me that she was the sixth daughter to own it and that it was passed down when a daughter gave birth to her first child. My mother wore the locket regularly, and when she gave it to me I suggested that I would be happy if she would continue to wear it because I wasn't quite ready for it. She did.

Then, a really bad thing happened: my parents' home in Melrose Park was burglarized while they were in Florida. The locket was gone, along with some other favorite, but not "valuable" jewelry pieces that had not been stored in the bank safety deposit box. You can imagine how we felt. My mother even told me that I should have kept it!

But some sad stories do have happy endings. I have the locket! My mother had actually put it somewhere "safe" before she went away for the winter, and of course it was hidden so completely that she forgot where it was. After her death, I found it tucked away in her closet. She would have been as thrilled to find it as I was.

36 LETTERS
and the Korman/Yesersky Engagement Contract

Embossment on Chaim's paper, about this size. The word, "CAPITOL," is printed under the image of the building.

The letters were translated by Mark Alsher (M.A.) in 2003. I have arranged them in chronological order with as much accuracy as possible. They are not all dated and some were written on the same days but in different locations.

They do not follow a regular "to and fro" pattern because of the time lost in transit; sometimes new letters were written before replies were received. Yente complained that a letter took two weeks to arrive (Letter 8), but considering that mail travelled on ships and Yente's own voyage from Bremen to New York City spanned a period from July 8 to July 18, 1905, two weeks seems a remarkable delivery time. The letters were postmarked both at their source and destination.

Most of the letters were written on very ordinary paper that would not be called fine stationery. Chaim often wrote on paper that was embossed with a colorless small image of a domed building, which I cannot identify, and was printed with pale blue lines; Yente's paper was plain and unlined. Some of the Russian letters are written on pre-stamped government postcards, but extra postage was added for the American destination. Chaim, Rose, and Joe Passman used business letterheads, and Rabbi Benjamin Korinman once used letterhead paper from a business where Chaim had been employed. No one wasted paper or postage and often a second or third family member added his own message to another's letter

They wrote with pens dipped into ink. You can see the flexibility of each pen nib in the variations of the line thickness that were produced by the pressure of the writer's hand. The look of each letter is very personal. It's also interesting to see how much style they put into addressing the envelopes in English, a language that was very foreign to them; they were accustomed to the alphabets of Yiddish, Hebrew, and Cyrillic Russian.

Letter 1

Translated from Yiddish. In this letter, Chaim writes using the formal second person (ir) and not the familiar form (du) that he uses in the other letters that he must have written later. This letter contains a lot of Russian words. (M.A.)

Capital, 11 July

Best friend Yente!

Yesterday I received your two letters from June 27 and from July 8. I had just come on the 8th in the evening and had a very good time on the trip. I can write you that when the king traveled back, he stopped at the station where we were. A transport of soldiers on their way to the east was waiting, so he got off to say good-bye to them, and I was standing on the platform then, so I saw him and the crown prince very well. Now they say that we will be going to the outposts very soon but where and when is not yet known. In the meantime, the service is going very well for us, thank God.

Esteemed Yente, I cannot describe for you how much I constantly think about you. Though you will indeed say why do I have to think about you. I am in my house with my parents. Nevertheless, I think a lot. What I think I will write to you. I have already thought about myself. Until now, I have also thought a lot about myself, because everything has been --- about me. But now everything will remain for as long as God allows. The time will come and it will again be thought about. In the worst case, I will serve for another 3 years though I have not yet lost hope, but I have to figure on this. But you are taking a very difficult thing on yourself. You have to quarrel with your parents this way for a time and you cannot yet go around to anybody, and holding it to yourself in your heart is very difficult, and, as I understand, you are too soft in this regard. About this I think about how to make it easier for you, but unfortunately I have no means for this.

But it seems to me that if I write to you it will make things easier for you. You should not anger your parents, and if a match is proposed to you, you should not refuse, because I am of the opinion that whatever is destined will come, and I think that you also feel this way, because whatever is destined to a person, no one can change. This is my opinion that I am writing. It is possible that it is not right, so you should write to me. Perhaps I am not writing correctly, but I ask you not to worry, because I am writing what I think, and perhaps I should not have written at all. I am writing because I cannot hide anything from you. I ask you once again write me. Perhaps you know how I can be of help to you so that you can be more calm.

There is, for the moment, no more news. Our --- are for the moment not set to go to the east. We are set to go as it will be needed to --- and to Karaol but what will be later cannot be known. In the meantime, no one knows what is going on under his shoulders.

Remain healthy from me your best good friend who wishes you all the best and writes to you all that he thinks.

Chaim.
Please answer

We no longer use the distinctions between formal and familiar when speaking English but these forms still exist in many languages. Formal forms are used to show respect, especially when speaking with persons of authority or those who are older. Familiar forms are appropriate for use with friends, family, and children.

The year is 1904.

Chaim probably wrote this letter in Smolensk, the capital of Smolensk Gubernia, where he was stationed in the Russian Army. The King he mentions in the letter is Czar Nicholas II, and the crown prince is his younger brother Mikhail. Nicholas's son Alexei was born soon after and replaced his uncle as heir. (M.A.)

The Russo-Japanese War had begun in February, 1904 and soldiers were being sent to Manchuria in the east.

Chaim is in his first year of military service and anticipating three more. He is not in a position to ask Yente to marry him.

Chaim writes "no one knows what is going on under his shoulders." I think that this is a reference to the Russian government as "he" which is similar to referring to the government as "Fonye."(A further explanation of the name "Fonye" is attached to Letter 7.)

A person's heart is located "under his shoulders" and I suppose that Chaim means that no one knows what the government's intentions or future plans might be.

Letter 2

Chaim may be indicating that he will be leaving Russia when he travels.

Smolensk Railway Station, 2005.
Wikimedia Commons.

This Yiddish letter is written using the formal form of address ("ir," you). Other letters from Chaim to Yente use the familiar form ("du," thou). (M.A.)

Best friend Yente,

I come to inform you that I came home, and I feel much better, thank God. I rested a little, and you can be calm. I think I will travel on Sunday or Monday. Before going, I will write you a letter. I cannot write any more now, because the [Sabbath] candles are already being blessed. Remain healthy and happy.

From me, your best good friend who wishes and hopes to hear all good things from you.

Chaim

Regards from the depths of my heart to your parents and your household from me, the above mentioned.

Letter 3

Translated from Yiddish. The last line on page four is missing. (M.A.)

This letter was written after Chaim departed Russia.

Yente has accompanied Chaim as far as Berestovitza, which is now known as Vyalikaya, in Belarus. This town is about 10 miles north of Svisloch.

Chaim has continued his journey west through Bialystok, a town now located in Poland.

Svislotsh, November 23

Best friend Chaim!

Now our correspondence is beginning again. May God grant that we indeed hear good things one from another, that all good things shall begin for us. Esteemed Chaim, I have duly received all of your letters and telegrams. I thank you very much for your accuracy. The reason we telegraphed from Brisk when you left us is because we did not receive any letters.

We received your letter Sunday evening; therefore we were very worried about your health. When I came back from Berestovitza Station, I was nagged for not accompanying you as far as Bialystok. You can imagine my situation then, and my parents did not let me say one word, but only shouted that I am not a mentsh [an honorable, decent person]. I don't go into another person's situation. They said that you should not let me go, so I should also have gone, and my father was also troubled by the fact that he did not go himself with you. But my pain then was baseless. But now I hope that it will be good. It is said that the person who sows with tears will reap with song. So shall it be with us.

A time will come when we will recall everything with pleasure. I already have pleasure in knowing that you are free. We have no obstacles, and as for material things, God can help. We don't intend to live a princely life. We will live as God helps, as long as it is in freedom and contentment.

Yente begins with the location, Svisloch, and the date, written in Russian, and continues her letter to Chaim in Yiddish.

You should not work extremely hard because health is more valuable than anything. First of all rest, then you will see what you have to do. Now I can write you that I am in the best of health, may God grant you no worse. I have improved. I think I will begin to sew. Meanwhile, I sit at home and I make what I need for myself. My mother also makes everything that I need. But she says that what she makes is not for me but for Chaim. She says that she loves you more than me.

But it pleases me very much that my thoughts are equal to my parents'. Now I am not bothered by anything. It seems to me that I have attained my goal. Imagine before when I used to recall (in fact it never left my thoughts) where you were, and what could happen to you, that means with me also, and that would not allow me to be calm, not during the day, not at night. But now you are free. It seems to me that I need nothing more.

Gitl is very mad at me for not telling her anything. Strangers are talking, and they ask her, and she knows nothing. She says that I am hiding things from her. I answered her that I do not know anything. Perhaps strangers know better, and if there were anything to tell, I would surely tell her.

Remain healthy and happy, as is wished for and expected of you by your Yente.

My parents and also the children send their warm regards and expect good news from you --- My parents thank you for the regards. [They] will write you a letter when you ---

Yente and her mother are sewing for her trousseau. Bed linens and household items would have been made at home, as well as clothing. Girls were usually taught dress-making skills and most also had the ability to do the various styles of embroidery that were used to embellish bed and table linens. (Yente's cross-stitch embroidery patterns were found with her letters.) A girl often prepared a collection of items that she would need as a married woman, before her engagement. Here, Yente and her mother acknowledge that Chaim is the intended bridegroom, even before the formal engagement contract has been signed.

The Gitl Yente mentions in her letter is her friend Gitl Slutsky.

Letter 4

Translated from Yiddish, except for the greetings, first and last lines of Benjamin Korinman's letter, and the greeting of Yechezkel's letter, which are in Hebrew. (M.A.)

The secular date is December 5, 1904.

This letter was written to Chaim while he was "at the ship" and waiting to leave for America. The ship that took him from Europe to New York departed from Antwerp, but he may have taken a ship to Antwerp from a port closer to Brest. It is also possible that he travelled to Antwerp overland by rail.

There was often a quarantine period for travelers and Chaim was probably either in this holding stage or simply waiting for the next ship.

Rabbi Korman refers to "cards," which are postcards, commonly used at that time.

I do not know anything about Yankev Pitikovsky.

Yoyl and Velvyl are Benjamin's brothers.

With the Help of God Almighty
Tuesday, of the week of the Torah reading Miketz
28 Kislev, second day of Hanukah, 5665
Brisk

Peace and blessing to my dear and cherished son Mr. Chaim Km, may he live,

First I inform you that we are all, thank God, healthy and peaceful. May God grant us to hear from you only good tidings and consolations in all matters physical and spiritual, Amen.

Second, I write you that I have received the four cards which you have sent me up until now. The fourth card especially was read with much delight. Thank God you are already at the ship, and you should not worry at all and not be unsettled. God Almighty who has helped you up until now will not abandon you in the future and probably what has happened has been for the best with God Almighty's help.

But you should direct yourself to go in a good path and strengthen yourself in Judaism and in all matters in general as you have done until now. Better is certainly good. And you should especially be very, very careful to observe the Sabbath as it has to be. And for God's sake, you should not listen to the talk of such people, wicked people, with the evil inclination to be as they want to convince you [to be], and who offer you much good fortune if you were not to observe the Sabbath and depart from Judaism, and they will explain [things] to you, with false arguments. I inform you, for God's sake, for God's sake, you should not pay attention to them and not take their advice. You should strengthen yourself very much, and you will defeat them and withstand the temptation and remain with Judaism. You should know that all good fortune comes only from God Almighty, to whomever He wants, He gives. Therefore, you should strengthen yourself very much and be sure of the help of God Almighty, and this will be my entire consolation and dearer than much good.

And that which you wrote in the third card that you brought to the ship another four rubles and 50 kopeks, I write you that I claimed this here from Yankev Pitikovsky, and that which you insulted him in the three cards, I write you that you did not have to. He confided in me that he [is] not so far wrong. Yoyl and Velvyl and their wives have already come, and according to how it appears they are not making any great fortunes there.

You should write me letters every week. This will be my consolation. From me, your father, who seeks your peace and pleads for you and awaits the salvation,

Binyomin Korinman.

I also seek the peace of my dear friend, the esteemed Mr. Shimon Fine (?), and my dear friend, the esteemed Mr. Chaim Tsvi Fine (?), and my dear friend, the esteemed Mr. Tsvi Hirsh Sidelnik with all of their households.

Blessed is the Lord
Tuesday, 23 November, Brest
Dear and gentle Chaim, dear one,

I read your greeting. Thank God you are already at that point. I know that you are healthy, thank God. May the dear God grant that you arrive at that place healthy and also arrive in a good time. May good fortune await you there. You need have no evil eye at your departure. Many like you are traveling. May God just give you health, and in America you will also do well.

I ask you, dear Chaim dear, to write me about your journey, and when you arrive, write to me at Kayle's in detail of what happens to you. May God grant that this letter reaches you in the best of health, your devoted Leah who hopes for your good fortune,

Leah Merke.

To my dear brother Mr. Chaim Korman,

I also come to inform you that I and my wife and little children are, thank God, healthy. Only one thing is not so good - that there is no livelihood. There is no more news to write.

From me, your devoted brother,
Yekhezkel Korman.

Write out a correct address. And you should describe how things go for you, the journey. Write out everything.

Letter 5

Translated from Yiddish (M.A.)

Svislotsh, 29 December

Dear Chaim!

I received your letter today and read it with the greatest delight. Imagine my joy that you can now earn your livelihood and you can study. You do not have to feel bad at all that you cannot get more. When God wants it, the small becomes big and the big small.

I see now more piously. For both of us, a few months ago, we did not know what was happening to us, not only that you were not earning anything, but you were not free. You were in the hands of another. And I aspired to something which I could not reach, and no person could help me, only God. So I hope to God

Leah Merke may be Benjamin's sister Leah, Chaim's aunt, as she writes on Benjamin's letter.

I do not know who Kayle is.

The Evil Eye is one of the most powerful and frightening of Jewish superstitions. The Evil Eye exists in many forms and they are all equally significant. "Kein ayain hora" is Yiddish for "no evil eye." The words are often slurred together as "kenahora" and said following a compliment, such as,"What a lovely baby, kenahora!"

When Yente mentions that Chaim was" in the hands of another," she is referring to the Russian Army—not another woman!

Yente asks Chaim to have his photograph taken in the cabinet card format. Cabinet cards are photographs mounted on a heavy card stock, about 4" x 6", and often with an imprint of the photographer and location just below the photograph. The cards were popular in both Russia and America.

Blume, is Bessie Priluker, Yente and Rochl's (Yente's sister Rose) cousin. Bessie is living with Rose and Harris Brody in Philadelphia.

that he will continue to help us. Do not work very hard because your health is more dear to me than everything, not only money.

Dearest Chaim, you write that you will get photographed. I ask you not to do anything different, and I allow myself the pleasure of telling you that you should get photographed right away, only cabinet cards, and send for Aunt Chaye also.

Now I must admit to you that I miss [you] very much. Perhaps if I were to have one card, I would be happier, because now, not one thing in the world is a pleasure for me except your letters which I read several times a day. Do not spare the few rubles for me, and photograph yourself as soon as you receive this letter.

Now I can write you some news that our Rokhl and Blume have written that they are anxiously awaiting you, and they are very happy that we will be in America. They think that you will travel to Philadelphia. Rokhl writes that she is expecting me with the greatest delight. When she considers that I will be in America, she cries for joy. If God leads, we will be together, but I am happier that you are settling in New York rather than in Philadelphia. I think that it is good to be together for a visit but not all the time, and may God help that we can travel one to another in joy. My father is also writing today to the children, so I am writing to Rokhl for her to write and tell me what is necessary in America for me for the household and what is worthwhile to take. I will gradually order, because later it will be difficult all at once.

Remain healthy and happy, as wishes you your Yente.

My parents send their regards and wish you all the best. Also all of our children send their regards and expect to hear good letters from you. I told them that you would send your photograph, so they don't stop talking about you all day, from me, your devoted Yente.

Letter 6

Translated from Yiddish. (M.A.)

Svislotsh, 10 January

Dear Chaim!

I wonder very much why I have not received a letter from you for so long. I don't know what to think. I don't sleep at night. Maybe you are, God forbid, not healthy. I always ask that you write me a few words because I am very concerned. I go to the post office every day, and I come home with nothing. I can't get myself to do anything. Please, my dearest, write me often. I understand your condition, that things are difficult for you, but I can't make it better. In the meantime, the letters are my hope and delight. In such a time, one can imagine all sorts of ideas, thinking unwillingly, when one is so upset. Especially since I have not received any letters, I don't know what to think.

This week we hired a Christian woman, because my mother was having a hard time managing alone. I am not doing anything in the house now, because I am busy with myself, so it is difficult without a maid. Also, write me what your parents write you from Brisk, also your brother and uncles. Perhaps you would write to your parents that they should come to us. I would like that very much. My parents also request this, to see the in-laws. And write me in detail what is happening with you and whether you will remain for a long time with your cousin.

Remain healthy and happy, as wishes you your eternally devoted Yente. I ask you one more time, write often. I will always answer you right away with the greatest appreciation. Believe me that it has eaten me up waiting for letters more than writing to you. But what can you do? It is all from God, and now we can indeed hope that an end will begin. It is sooner than before.

Remain healthy, from me, the above-mentioned.

Yente asks if Chaim will continue to stay with his cousin, who is probably Joseph Passman.

Letter 7

Translated from Yiddish. (M.A.)

New York, 16 January

Dear Yente!

I have received your letter and read your letter with much joy. A few days earlier I had been troubled because by my calculation I should have received an answer on Saturday. Unfortunately, I did not receive it. I received it today, Monday. Forgive me for not writing you a letter earlier, not waiting for an answer. The reason for this is as follows. Earlier, I was going around and I did not know where in the world I was. Later, when I had gotten a place, I expected an answer from you.

Now I want to write you about my work. I am studying to be a cutter and designer (a cutter is what we call a "zakroyshtsik") in a business of ready-made underwear (and designer is the one who makes the form by which to cut.) It is cut out of paper, and afterwards the cutter cuts according to the papers. It is a very fine job and good work. You can earn a lot at that work. I paid 50 dollars for the teaching, and learning will take two months. I am not studying in school but I am learning in a business by experience, because in school studying lasts a long time and they only teach design, and afterwards, after completing the course, I would have to look for a place to work, and here where I am studying to be a cutter I am already getting 7-8 dollars a week from the start. And they are always raising this, and when I have finished learning design, I can then earn good money. But I don't expect great fortunes from the start. Whatever God does, and I hope that God will help us.

I am doing everything with diligence, and I always say that I am fortunate that I am through with Fonye [Russia], not so much just from military service but

Chaim is describing his new trade. He will become a cutter and designer in the garment industry. A cutter actually cuts the fabric and a designer is the pattern-maker, which requires much more skill than working as a stitcher or presser. "Form" is another word for "pattern."

The sum of $50 in 1904 is comparable to $1250 now. Chaim had paid about $30 for his passage to New York. In paying for the teaching, he has made a significant investment in his future.

Chaim's immigration documents show that he arrived in New York with $10. It's very likely that he had not declared all that he had brought.

Chaim refers to "Fonye" as if he were a person. Fonye is Yiddish for Ivan ... so all gentiles were called Fonye—sort of like "Joe Blow" or " John Doe." The letters "v" and "f" are often exchanged in linguistics, so Ivan becomes Ifan and the "I" drops off leaving "fan." The vowel sounds "a" and "o" are often used interchangeably in Slavic languages (Moscow is pronounced Mascow). So now we have Fon ... and "nye" at the end is a diminutive ending, sort of like "nyu" in mamenyu or tatenyu–hence fonye.

Explained by Paul Azaroff and shared by Martin Zafman.

"Gitl" refers to Yente's friend Gitl Slutsky.

Chaim says that a pledge may be made. He refers to an engagement contract, the tenaim. It is both a legal contract and a public ceremony.

Leyele is Yente's brother Lazar.

I do not know why Moyshe would be in Svisloch. Perhaps he also worked for the railroad. If his aunt lived in Svisloch, Chaim would have spent Passover of 1903 with his aunt and uncle.

from him entirely. I thank and praise the Most High that he freed me from Fonye and hope that God will not forsake us. Now I am not worried at all. In the beginning I was a little homesick. Now I have thought it out and considered that it must be this way. It cannot be otherwise, and everything in its time.

Now, it pleases me very much that you write that my uncles were at your place. I already had a letter from home. Last week I got a letter from Uncle Yoyl. He wrote me that they visited your house, and he wrote that he liked your house, a very fine family. And today I got a letter from Father. He writes that Yoyl and Velvyl were in Svisloch, and from what they told him, he is pleased with the match. Therefore, I should write and tell him if I send letters to you and how things are with me. I should not be ashamed and should write him everything. But I had nothing and did not know what to write because it is still very early. I am far from settled, and I am not yet working on my own. I do not yet earn any money. I have now been working for eight days. I work from 8 a.m. until 6 p.m. I am learning the work very well. I think that I will learn it in two months, but they won't pay me until after two months, and afterwards, when I am earning money, one cannot so quickly …

… Now how could I answer his question? But now, after your question, I can give an answer to my father. You write me that everyone in the town says that we have made a match, and when you are asked, you don't know what to say, and Gitl is angry with you that you don't tell her. She is right, but I don't fault you. And regarding the question which you ask whether you should tell Gitl, it seems that there is nothing to hide, but surely you should not yet. From this I have some pains, but you are absolutely not at fault. You are correct. You cannot know what is in my heart, though you know me a little. But you cannot know, so I wrote my father that he should correspond with your father, and if they require that a pledge be made, let it be done. Then you will be able to answer freely if you are asked who, and you will be able to tell Gitl, and you will be able to tell everyone.

About myself, I can write you that I am healthy, thank God, may God grant that we hear the same from you. I have already bought a suit for Passover. There is no more news to write. Remain healthy and happy, have a happy Passover. Remember last Passover and you will know how happy you should be that God has helped us that we are through with Fonye for good, and He will probably also help us further. From me, your eternally beloved, who hopes to see you very soon, and wishes you health and happiness and a happy Passover.

Yours, Chaim

Regards to your parents from the depths of my heart. Regards also to Leyele. Warm regards to all of the children. Today I got a card from Moyshe, my aunt's [husband]. They thank me for the card. I ask you, my dear, give them my regards. I thank them for writing. I would write them myself, but I don't have the time.

Letter 8

Translated from Yiddish. The dots, where things seem to be left unsaid, are in the original. (M.A.)

Svisloch, 20 January

Dear Chaim!

I received your letter today, read it with great delight. I should actually not answer you immediately. I should have done what you do, not write anything for three weeks. Afterwards, the letter takes two weeks, so it comes to five weeks waiting for one letter, and you maintain that we should be okay with that, since whatever comes about with more difficulty is more dear, but I don't think that way. And secondly I am a good person, not as bad a one as you. But I think that it won't be like this any more, therefore I forgive you. I wrote you a letter last week, how things were in my heart, but you deserved it for me to berate you even more but ... I was so upset that I do not want to remember what I was thinking. You apologize, saying that you had nothing to write. Do I require news from you? You did not have anything to do. This can be understood, that when a person arrives, he can't just immediately start doing something, but must consider very well what to do, and I do not require any fortunes from you. But I am concerned about your health.

Dear Chaim, I am very happy that you get frequent letters from home. Also that your father is going to correspond with my father. We will surely invite him to us, because my parents want it very much. What you write about the clothes, our Rokhl sent me forms from Philadelphia, and I asked her about other things. I have not yet received an answer.

Everything is fine with us. We are healthy, thank God. I am very happy that you don't miss Russia, if what you write is true. You really should write a letter to Aunt Chaye, because she is always asking about what you write and whether you are pleased with America.

Concerning what you write that your uncle may ask about ... How I should know what to say, I don't understand. I cannot write. Perhaps your letters are read, but you can receive the letters yourself.

I am going to sew a little. My teacher is pleased with me and says that I will soon know what she does. There is no special news here with us.

Remain healthy and happy, as is wished for and expects of you,
your dear Yente.

My parents and also the children send you their warm regards and expect frequent and good letters from you...

Yente mentions that Rose has sent her "forms" from Philadelphia; these are dress patterns designed in the American style. Yente has been taking sewing lessons.

I do not know if Chaya is Chaim's aunt or Yente's.

Yente is concerned about the questions that Chaim's uncle may ask her parents. They will probably inquire about plans for a formal engagement contract, the tenaim, *and what the Yeserskys will give Yente as a dowry. They will also be interested in the Yesersky ancestry and will be impressed by famous scholars such as Rabbi Yehuda Low Halevi Edel, Solomon's great-grandfather. Perhaps they will discover that renowned Rabbi Isaac Elchanan Spector, who taught and ordained Rabbi Benjamin Korinman at the Kovno Yeshiva, was married to a Yesersky.*

This letter is from Rose to her parents. She and her family are planning Yente's needs for America even before the engagement.

The Brody letterhead shows that the stables are on Tasker Street and his residence is on Greenwich Street. The two properties were adjoining and their home was directly south of the business.

A samovar. *Courtesy of Aimee Delman.*

A samovar was the centerpiece of the table in a Russian home, around which life revolved, and drinking tea from the samovar was a way of life. A traditional samovar consists of a large metal container with a faucet and a metal pipe running through the center. The pipe is filled with solid fuel to heat the water in the surrounding container. A teapot is placed on top and is used to brew a strong concentrate of tea. The tea is served by diluting this concentrate with boiling water from the main container at a ratio of about 10 parts water to one part tea concentrate. The base metal for a samovar was always brass, although it could be plated with gold or silver. Most were small, about 18 inches high.

Rose wrote that there was an American custom that a ship's ticket should be purchased locally and sent to the individual making the voyage. She may have been referring to the role of the "immigrant bank" in her neighborhood. These banks were commercial enterprises, started mainly by established German Jews. They were places where recent immigrants could save money and arrange to buy steamship tickets to bring their families to America. It was also possible to purchase this transportation in Russia where the steamship lines advertised and sold tickets.

Letter 9

Translated from Yiddish. It is unsigned. This letter contains a number of English words ("letter," "presents"). The writer (I assume it is Rokhl) began to write the word "street," then crossed it out and wrote the Yiddish word for street ("gas").
This is the letter written on the stationery of Harris Brody, Boarding and Livery Stables for Rent, on Tasker St. (M.A.)

Philadelphia, January 29, 1905

Dearest Parents,

I have duly received your letter. It pleases me very much that we will have Yente also in America, half of our family. Now I already have a hope that you, my dear parents, will also one day be together with us.

You ask me what she needs in America. Since everything in America costs half the price, for a dollar you can buy a lot of things. For a half dollar here you can buy the most beautiful shirt. That which she has from before, she should bring with her, but to go now and sew is not worthwhile. In America, when you go out in the street, everything is before your eyes. Since everything is very cheap, no matter what you have, you must buy. But she should bring linens with her, a little ---, a samovar, all of that is expensive here. Handwork is also not necessary, but she should bring what she has, because in America she will not make this. Here, time is expensive. For money, everything is made with a machine. Because of that, it is cheap.

Copper is not so much in style because it is absolutely not necessary in America. For 50 cents (kopeks) you can get the biggest and nicest pot. Here, pots are blue and white. Here, the style is that when a person marries, presents are sent from the family and a house is fixed up with everything.

Yente does not have to get anything else until Korman sends her a ship's ticket. It would be better for her to return the money to him because in America there is a custom that he has to send her a ticket. Write Korman that he should come down to us on a Sunday. Send him our address. Sunday people don't work, so we will be able to arrange everything for the trip. She should bring a very big samovar. I have a new, small samovar, so I will trade it with her here and I will pay her the additional amount.

Letter 10

Translated from Yiddish. Some lines are missing on the copy of the original letter. (M.A.)

Dear Yente,

I read your letter with much delight, and what I wrote you in the previous letter that I would be earning my livelihood right away and that I would be able to study - nothing came of that because it was not worth my laboring for a long time. But now I am learning to be a cutter and designer, that is a "zakroyshtsik" who makes the forms by which to cut, and when I have learned the work well, I will be able to make a nice living because it is very good work and clean work. I work from eight until six o'clock, and when I come from work, after eating I go and ... which we need to have when I recall that a year ago I was not earning any money. I was sold to Fonye [the Czar] and he worked me and tormented me and I used to have to stand in freezing weather and storms at the post and guard duty and the question in my heart - for whom and why must I do this - tormented me even more. Now when I recall this, I jump for joy. I feel free. No one orders me about. I am not afraid of anyone, and we both have to be especially happy that God helped us out of Fonye, and nothing is spoiled for us.

Imagine my delight Yente when my father himself writes to me saying that if I write letters to Svisloch often, I should write and tell him what is written to me from Svisloch, and he writes me that I must not be ashamed and write everything to him. So I wrote him that he should correspond with your father, and if you require a match to be made, then they should make a match, because we have already spoken ourselves. So now let our parents make a match, so they won't act like strangers, and you yourself won't be ashamed to tell people when they ask about me, and I will have delight from you all, and further, I will be able to write a letter to your parents also.

You also ask me to send tickets. I say that I will take off this Shabbes or next Shabbes, because all week I have no time, but on Shabbes I have it. If it is nice weather I will take off because this week there is very bad freezing weather and snowstorms. Yesterday there was a snowstorm all day so you couldn't even go out on the street, and today there is freezing weather. I am sitting and writing the letter, and my hand is frozen, so I cannot hold the pen. I am further happy that your sisters are expecting us and that they are happy that we are coming to America, and I am also happy that I am settling in New York.

You did well in writing to Rokhl telling her to write and tell you what to prepare, because in America they don't use a lot of things that cost a lot at home …

I would like to write you more, I am very cold, so I cannot write. May everyone remain healthy, from me, Your devoted

Chaim.

Please answer immediately. Regards to your parents also. Regards to Leyele and all of the children also.

I wanted to write you a little about what we hear about Fonye, what is happening in Russia. I will write that in the next letter.

The word "Fonye," as explained in Letter 7, refers to the Russian government, the Czar, the Army. Chaim does not mean that he was actually "sold," but he feels the army owned him.

Chaim writes that his father is willing to make a match. The match refers to the engagement contract, and by celebrating at the engagement ceremony, the parents will not remain strangers.

Chaim mentions Yente's sisters. She has one sister in Philadelphia, but Chaim must be including cousin Bessie, who is like a sister, and is living with the Brodys.

Blockaded Cars on 23rd Street, New York, 1905. This is probably the aftermath of the snowstorm Chaim described in his letter. *Library of Congress, Detroit Publishing Company Collection.*

Leyele is Lazar Yesersky, who is six years younger than Chaim. There are five other children younger than Lazar.

Chaim would have read about events in Russia in the New York Yiddish newspapers. Even The New York Times and other English-language newspapers reported on the Russo-Japanese War, the strikes, and the pogroms.

Letter 11

Translated from Yiddish. The word, "Fonye," refers to the Czar. Yente is probably referring to the draft. (M.A.)

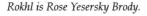

Rokhl is Rose Yesersky Brody.

Svislotsh, 30 January

Dear Chaim!

I duly received your letter from the 26th. Read it with much delight. Dearest Chaim, it appears that you know me very little because you apologize to me because you are not yet earning money. That would have been fitting had I, when you were leaving Russia, made you promise no less than that as soon as you would arrive in America, you should immediately earn money. It seems to me that, to the contrary, I said to you that you should not immediately take up any difficult work, and consider what is best for you, and when you would determine this to be good work, I would be very pleased, because you are there and not among strangers. Usually your cousins advised you how good it is. You write that in America it is very cold. See to it that you take care of yourself and not, God forbid, catch cold.

In the previous letter, you wrote that you wrote to your parents that they should correspond with us, but until now we have not received any letters. Perhaps they don't know our address.

Last week we got a letter from our Rokhl. She asks what we hear from you, because they know nothing about you. You haven't visited them, also not written. So we wrote her what's doing with you. I also thank you for fulfilling my request and having yourself photographed. I anxiously await your card. I promised Gitele your photograph. I told her that you were having your picture taken.

Ask your female cousins whether --- is not more expensive than in Russia, whether it is worthwhile to bring it, because, if it is more expensive, I will buy a few more things. My mother gives me, but if in America it is expensive more would be bought for me. You should write me, for God's sake, because I need to know this. And I won't ask this of Rokhl. My grandmother promised to give me a little bit of silver, a ---.

Write me how much you have to study in order to know the work. Dear Chaim, you write that you are pleased that you are rid of Fonye. You can imagine that I am even more pleased than you, because from a distance the matter is even more terrible. Last year when there used to be a frost, I couldn't rest when I used to ask myself what is with you now. Even now in America we don't have to concern ourselves as much. You are, after all, free. Nevertheless, I am not calm. This is such a characteristic that from a distance everything seems worse, and I cannot, for the time being, be pleased. I am very pleased that you are with a cousin of yours, because this is surely in a family home. You should, for God's sake, not eat in any restaurant. Also, write me whether you still smoke.

Remain healthy and happy, from me your always devoted Yente Yesersky.

My parents send you their warm regards. Also the children and we expect frequent and good letters from you. With us there is a battalion of soldiers because the seminarians made a rebellion, also the worker …

Hyman Korman with cigar in hand,
photographed by Fabian Bachrach, about 1962

Letter 12

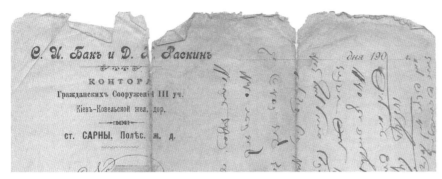

This is the letterhead of S.I. Bak & D.K.Raskin, Office of Civil Buildings, Section 3, Kiev Kovel Railroad, Station Sarny, Polesye Railroad. Chaim and his uncles were employed by the Polesye Railroad and Chaim worked in this office.

The old Russian was translated by Oleg Medvedevsky.

Translated from Hebrew. The last paragraph is translated from Yiddish. The dashes "---" are where words (and, in the last paragraph, an entire line) did not show up on my copy. The letter is written in a very nice, scholarly, flowery style, with many references to biblical verses. (M.A.)

With the Help of God the Almighty
Monday of the Torah reading Terumah
3 Adar 5665, Brisk

Peace and good wishes to my dear son, the beloved of my heart Mr. Chaim, may he live.

The secular date is Wednesday, February 8, 1905.

"Shiloh" and" the son of Peretz" are both references to the Messiah, each reference from different parts of the Bible.

First I will inform you that we are all, thank God, in good health. May God continue to grant this in the future, and may we see and hear from you only good news and tidings and comforts until Shiloh and the son of Peretz shall come, speedily in our days, Amen.

I received your letter on the last holy Sabbath with the attachment of the letter from my friend --- the dear soul, our teacher Rabbi Shimon Passman, and behold I saw there was a pamphlet folded double, written on both sides, and I ate up this scroll and it was as sweet as honey in my mouth, and I called the Sabbath a delight for how greatly was I delighted to hear that you are well and that the Lord has enabled you to find a place of rest where you earn your livelihood from clean and easy work, to study in the home of an honest man who keeps the Sabbath in the prescribed manner, and believe me my son that I cannot describe and depict for you the greatness of the delight and joy that was in all of our hearts here while reading the letter. Thank God for that.

Let's hope that you will surely, quickly reach your desired goal with God's help and come and see proven the words of the Psalmist who sang in the holy spirit: "Many are the thoughts in the heart of man, but the counsel of the Lord shall stand." For who would have believed in days gone by, at the time when you were in the "Raskin" office, if a man, a prophet who knew the future or a dreamer of dreams would then have come to us and would have said to us, behold days shall come in a year or two and Zakarushchik will be in America for they would surely have spit in his face. And now our eyes see that the matter has come to light from the One who causes all causes as our rabbis of blessed memory said in the

Chaim had worked in the Raskin office (see the letterhead at the beginning of this letter). It was the office where housing for the railroad workers was planned and designed. While this experience did not prepare him to become a zakarushchik, a tailor, it certainly did prepare him for his career as a builder in Philadelphia.

Near Sarny along the Kiev-Kovel Railroad in the Ukraine.

The Pentateuch a name for the first five books of Moses, the Torah.

Rabbi Shlomo Yitzhaki, better known by the acronym Rashi (February 22, 1040–July 13, 1105), was the author of the first comprehensive commentaries on the Talmud, Torah, and Tanakh (the Hebrew Bible). His work is still studied today.

The Bible states in Leviticus 21:5," They shall not make baldness upon their head, neither shall they shave off the corners of their beard, nor make any cuttings in their flesh." Orthodox Jewish tradition takes this to mean that a man may not shave his beard with a razor with a single blade, since the cutting action of the blade against the skin "mars" the beard. This is Rabbi Korman's concern. Now some Orthodox Jews permit the use of scissors and certain electric shavers.

Benjamin scolds Chaim, but forgives him. Benjamin felt it was not up to the children to arrange their marriage; the match should have involved the parents. And Chaim should not have kept his plans secret from his father.

This is a section of the letter meant for Shimon Passman, Joe Passman's father. I do not know exactly how they are related to Sarah Passman, Benjamin's mother. I also do not know if the Passmans are ordained rabbis or if Benjamin uses the title as an honorific.

Ethics of the Fathers, "Regard nothing as impossible, for you find no man that has not his hour and no thing which has not its place."

Therefore, my son, love the work that has fallen in your lot and do not be lazy in it but direct your eyes and your heart and all of your senses to learn the work quickly in all of its details and particulars entirely and then things will be good for you. But by God be extremely careful that your heart be not led astray after those people, the wicked ones who seduce and instigate, but distance yourself from their ways like a bowshot and only cling to honest people who walk in good paths and fix for yourself every day at least an hour to study the Pentateuch with Rashi's commentary and also to say chapters of Psalms every day, and on every Sabbath study Chayyei Adam or Kitzur Shulchan Aruch [codes of Jewish law] in the matters of the Sabbath laws.

Also be careful not to remove the beard with a razor, even with something like a razor is forbidden. I also send you congratulations since your Aunt Pesil the wife of Goldfarb has given birth to a male child and the circumcision was yesterday.

And concerning the matter of the match of Sislovitz, I do not at the moment have their address, therefore send me the address and, though in this you have gone beyond the limits of ethics and respect in that you kept this matter from me when you were here, for then I would have gone with you to Sislovitz, and it would have been done in a more pleasant way. You have acted foolishly. Nevertheless, I forgive you and I hold no grudge against you for childishness took hold of you and you imagined that I would prevent it. Therefore you were afraid to tell me. This is not the case, but, on the contrary I would have strengthened your hand in the matter in the best way possible for the main part of the matter seemed very good to me as others put it to me and described it.

There is no other news now, only wishes for life and peace from me, your father who seeks peace and good and much success for you, who sits and waits for your reply.

Binyomin Korinman

I also ask and request you to write me a letter every week, and at least a postcard each and every week. Not one week should be skipped, and you should not wait until you get a letter from me. Also write me once in a while with news about your behavior and the customs of the place and whether there are groups there for learning and if there are preachers and expounders. In general, write me about all matters. From me, the aforementioned.

Peace and all the best to my honorable friend and relative the scholar and gentleman, our teacher Rabbi Shimon Passman. After sending best wishes to him and his household, may they live, I give him many thanks for his interceding and labor on behalf of my son, may he live, to find a place to stay. And I was very pleased that my son lodges in your house and will surely behave in your house in the Jewish way, in the best manner, and how good it would be if you two would fix a time to study together on the holy Sabbath day and every day in a free moment. I bless you from the depths of my heart. May God grant that you go up higher and higher with much happiness and wealth and success as you wish yourself and your friend wishes, your relative Binyomin Korinman

And I send greetings to my friend and relative the scholar and gentleman, our teacher Rabbi Tsvi Passman and his household and to my friend and relative the scholar, our teacher Rabbi Tsvi Sidelik.

To my dear brother Mr. Chaim Korman.

I can inform you that we received your letter but it is surprising that you did not write the address of Sislovitz because no one knows your address. I asked Yoelik and Binyomin the carpenter and Ershl Pavin, and they do not know. Therefore you should immediately write out your correct address to Sislovitz and you should ---

You should further write about America, what news do you hear there and whether you have seen Dovid Bialkin. There is nothing to ... There is no news. Everything is the same as before and there is nothing for you to miss.

From me, your devoted brother Yechezkel Korman. My wife ---

Letter 13

Translated from Yiddish, except for the place name and date at the top and the final paragraph (from Lazar Yesersky), which are translated from Russian. (M.A.)

Svisloch, 6 February

Dear Chaim,

I duly received your letter of the 5th of February and read it with the greatest delight. I am very pleased that you have frequent letters from home. It is quite sensible what your father writes you, but I am doubtful that this can be maintained in America, but it has to be understood, and one has to live as it is possible. Two days earlier, we received a letter from our Rokhl. Mother asked her what is necessary in America. She wrote what for her is better. She wrote that in America everything is cheap. But I can send you her letter and you will read it yourself. But I did not wait for her answer. I bought everything. There is a young woman here who was in New York 8 years. She told me everything that is needed in America, so I made everything. Rokhl writes what is cheap, but to buy everything cheap, you also need a lot. If I would wait, I would, in fact, be given less, but now what's done is done.

Yente begins her letter with a reference to Rabbi Korman's letters and most likely to his pleas to Chaim concerning the proper way to lead a Jewish life. Yente seems to be moderate and practical in her suggestion that "one has to live as it is possible." I think she would have been considered to be Modern Orthodox; in America, Yente and Chaim became Conservative Jews.

I am very pleased that you will soon be earning, because when a man earns, he is more proud of himself and when one does not earn one loses courage. But you do not have to interest yourself in that you are not earning, because you will arrive at a career.

Your parents have not yet written to us. I don't know the reason. I think they do not know our address.

Rokhl requests that you go to them. When you can, go to them for a day and you will get to know them. Also to --- Rubin (?). They request your address, so I sent it to her. I am also sending you their address and half a letter from Rokhl, because the second half is also written to my Grandmother, so we will mail it in Rudne (?).

I can write you dear Chaim that when you were in Smolensk I did not miss you as much as now. But it cannot be done any better. Everything in its time.

Remain healthy and happy is the wish for you from your devoted Yente.

My parents send you their warm regards and expect good things from you. Also all of the children send regards and kiss you ... Yente.

Esteemed Ch. Korman,

I am very pleased with your achievements. I am very thankful for your greetings. I wish you further achievements. I remain your indisputable friend.

Lazar Yesersky

This photograph of Lazar Yesersky Isard was found on his 1923 U.S. Passport application.

Letter 14

Translated from Yiddish. The dashes --- appear where words were not visible on the copy.

New York March 5, 1905

Dear Yente,

I received your letter Friday evening (that was yesterday evening). I read the letter with great delight. I recalled how, a year ago, I used to receive letters from you mostly on Friday evenings, so I actually cried with joy.

Now I can write you that today I received a letter from my parents. They are all healthy, thank God. The reason that I had not received any letter from them for such a long time is because the letters were delayed on the way. They also write that they wanted to write to you, but they did not know the address. So now I have written them the address, and I told them that they will receive an answer from you, and you will ask them to come, so they will come directly to you. I also wrote them that they should not speak about a dowry until they have first spoken with you, and you will tell them. You must understand what I mean ...

You also should have read how my father writes to me and insults me a little because I did not tell him. When I came from Smolensk, he would have gone with me to you and would then have arranged everything. He writes me "that you were ashamed to tell me and that you thought that I would interfere with you. On the contrary, I would have helped you with all possibilities, and I would have been very pleased." But after all that, he forgives me. His says that I acted with childish understanding and is also pleased with that.

Both Chaim and Yente must have been very apprehensive about Rabbi Korman's reaction to the news that they had planned a match without his involvement. Chaim seems much relieved that he has received only a modest scolding.
(Letter 12)

68

Last week I sent you two cards, for you and for Aunt Chaya, and now I am sending you a button and my photograph also.

I am now earning good money, and I am constantly getting more experienced in my work, because the work is not easy to learn because various work comes about, and experience is the main thing. Much experience is needed. I have learned the work entirely, but I still have little experience. Practice is the main thing.

And again concerning what Rokhl writes you that nothing must be made since in America everything is very cheap, I also wrote you in the previous letter that a lot of things do not have to be made, because in America the same things are not worn as in Russia, but not as Rokhl writes that in America everything is cheap. For one dollar, a lot of things can be bought, and I am writing you to say that it is not entirely as she writes. In America, a dollar is spent, and no one pays any attention, so to her it seems that it is cheaper, because what is bought here for one dollar cannot be bought in Russia for one ruble, and she forgets entirely that our dollar is worth two of your rubles.

Now, again, you write that Rokhl asks for me to come to them. They first have to write me a letter and ask that I come, and aside from that, I also have no time because I work on Sunday and not on Saturday, and Saturday they are surely busy.

Also that which Rokhl writes that you do not have to leave until I send you a ship ticket --- that you should preferably return the money to me --- I do not understand what she means by that whether she means to prevent your asking her for a ship ticket, or whether she means to protect you, because, after all, she does not know me, she wants a safeguard from me, and it is in fact a great safeguard. I cannot know what she means. You have to know ---,

Why don't you write to me? You do not write me at all about this. I wait for your writing.

Again, about traveling, first everything must also be considered. For the time being, I cannot marry you, because from my present earnings, no living can be made. It will take a little more time until I work myself up. You cannot hurry things, but must have patience. But I reckon that if it is agreeable to you to stay for a bit of time with Rokhl it would be --- You should leave after Passover and there you could learn a little English writing and speaking and we could see each other all the time until we understand that we can--- make a living Then write me your --- in that.

I am in the best of health. May God grant hearing the same from you. Stay healthy and happy. Enjoy yourself. This is my wish, from me, your dear Chaim.

Regards to the parents and the children from the depths of my heart. Special regards to --- I thank him very much for the greetings which he wrote me. I sent a letter to Aunt Chaya last week. Adieu.

Chaim writes that he is sending Yente cards and buttons. These are photographs—formal portrait cabinet cards and a photograph pinback button to be worn on clothing. See the illustration on page 72.

Pop was always generous with others and frugal with himself. He lived nicely, but modestly. I once heard him joke that he did not spend lavishly because he did not have a "rich father."

At this time, Chaim is working in New York and trying to save to marry Yente. Rose is married to Harris Brody, a very wealthy man, and Chaim is trying to warn Yente that things do not come cheaply in America.

Chaim is correct: from 1898–1914, one silver ruble was equal to $0.514 US gold dollars.

Chaim Korman, on a cabinet card, photographed in 1905 at Hurwitz's Studio of Art Photography, New York.

Letter 15

The money Yente mentions is her dowry. She is also receiving gifts of household items that she will bring to America.

Svislotsh, March 20th

Dear Chaim!

I received your letter today and read it with much delight. I am especially pleased that you had a letter from your parents because I was very disturbed when you wrote that you had not received a letter from them. I am also pleased that they will visit us.

I know that you write to your parents about money. They should ask me first, and I can write you that they say that money will surely be given to me, but not as much as would be given in Russia. But how much, I do not yet know exactly. Further, people are giving me very nicely. The point of what is given is not that it cost little, but rather that it be good. In the previous letter you wrote that I should not buy a lot of – but that if I can take money in place of it, I should take it. First of all, I don't know if I will be given more money than is figured, and second, this is better to me than money, because what is needed is sometimes better than money. I will not begrudge myself buying it, and if I bring it I will have --- What I buy here for 2 rubles I won't be able to buy there for any amount of dollars, and this is the sort of thing which is always worth money. It does not go out of style and it doesn't break. If money is lacking, it is more necessary than anything, but if not, then this is also money.

Also, when you write that you don't understand what RokhI means by writing me that you should send me a ship's ticket, you think bad of her. She means nothing by that, but is just writing what the style is. And in her opinion it is much nicer for me to be sent for. You are sending for me, not that I am going on my own to you.

Rokhl may consider Chaim younger because she is a married woman. Actually he is three years her senior.

You also write that Rokhl must write to you to invite you to them. First of all, she did not at first know the address and secondly, she considers you younger so perhaps she is waiting for you to write to her first. I am also pleased that you do not work on Shabbes, but they, I think, also don't work on Shabbes, because theirs is such a business that doesn't require working on Shabbes. But concerning your going to them, this interests me very much. At least, if you go it is certainly good, and, if not, do as you think best.

Now I can write you my opinion about my going to America. It seems to me that I will go a couple of weeks after Passover, because then the time is better. It is not very hot and not cold and some familiar people will also be traveling, and when I am at Rokhl's, she will be very pleased with that, and, as you write, I will learn the language a little which is a very good thing. Now imagine how we will be close to one another, and I have cousins in New York so I can come there and you can come once for a Shabbes to me. This will be worth very much to me. Secondly, I am now neither here nor there because I think more about there, so it is no longer pleasant to be where it no longer interests me. Every person must have an interest in life, and I am living in Russia without an interest. Therefore I think that one has to aspire to where the thoughts lead.

Letter 16

Translated from Yiddish (M.A.)

New York March 22

Dear Yente!

I duly received your letter today and read it with great delight. Imagine, today is Purim, we are sitting at the meal and I recall how I was a year ago. I feel fortunate enough, but out of sorts. We sat and had a very good time, but I was sad. I was also troubled that I had not received a letter from you because, by my calculation, I should have received a letter a few days earlier, and while thinking this way about you, the letter was brought in to me. I immediately opened the letter and read it with much joy. Everyone recognized that I was very pleased with the letter.

And that which you write me, my dear, that you are sick of the correspondence, you can imagine that I am no less sick of it. I can tell you that I myself never thought that I would yearn so much, but what can you do? Everything has its time. It is sooner rather than later.

Now, what you write me about wanting to travel after Passover together with familiar people is not a bad idea. I have already written you in the previous letter that I would very much want you to come after Passover. First, because I miss you very much, and further because you would become a little bit familiar with the country, learn a little writing and speaking. But only if it were agreeable to you to stay with Rokhl, because, you understand, I cannot have you stay with me yet. And now, according to my understanding of your letter, it is agreeable to you to stay with Rokhl, so it is best for you to travel after Passover and we will be able to see each other.

The trip from New York to Philadelphia is 2 hours and we will be near each other, and what you ask about baggage is now no worse than it was. Linen and underwear is also allowed in, so long as it is washed, not new, and other things have to be hidden where they will not be seen. A lot of things can be hidden in the linen and also you can keep things on yourself. And they don't inspect very carefully. It is as it once was. But no extra things have to be brought.

You write that you plan to be in Bialystok. You want to sew something for yourself. I don't understand why you need to sew for yourself. Homemade things are not used here.

Write to me about what you think about a ship ticket, whether you have written to Rokhl for her to send you one or whether you will buy it yourself or if you want me to send one to you. You don't write me, but Rokhl wrote. It doesn't matter to me, but I would only like to know what she means by that and whether she knows that I have money. But if you write that I should send, I will also surely send. But it is a very difficult thing for me because the ship ticket has to be to Philadelphia. Also, you have to know in which office to buy it, because you can

Chaim would benefit from his cousins' American experience, but he cannot confide in them until the engagement is official.

always be tricked. There are plenty of swindlers in America, and I cannot tell my cousins. Therefore it is very difficult for me, and it won't be any cheaper.

You surely have to get a government passport. It is very bad to travel without a government passport. For you it is surely not a good idea to steal across the border.

The reason my parents had not written is because they did not know your address. They are all healthy, thank God. I think that they have already written to you. You will surely invite them to your house. They will come right away and will make ---. Let it be just the same as if I were at home. I send the first congratulations. May we live happily, and may our parents derive pleasure from us.

Yente has asked Chaim to send photographs of himself. Here he tells her that he has sent two cabinet cards as well as three photographic buttons. The pinback button had been developed in the late 19th century and used as an advertising tool. Buttons also became a popular way to share personal photographs. Usually a single portrait was used and the button worn as jewelry.

I could send no more than two cards. I also sent you three buttons with my photograph. You wear them on yourself. I am worried --- maybe the cards will not arrive because they were sent unregistered. I myself had no time to go send them, so I gave it to my cousin. He sent it open as it was, to you and also the same to my parents. But I sent the buttons myself, registered.

Also concerning that which you write about not being pleased in that I don't keep my word, unfortunately I do, in fact, keep my word. We hear enough further news from Russia. My heart cries in me all day when I read in the paper how Jews are suffering in Russia and I am very disturbed by that. No more news is given.

An example of an early pinback portrait button, front and back. *Photograph courtesy of Beth Pulsipher Photography.*

May you all remain healthy and happy, from me, your devoted one, who hopes and wishes to see you soon. I am happy just thinking about it

Your devoted Chaim.

Leyele is Lazar; Velvele is William; and Tsirile is Celia.

Heartfelt regards to your parents. Regards to Leyele, the little brothers, also regards to the children. I ask you Yente to give a kiss to Velvele and Tsirile for me. At some time I will return it to you. Adieu

Letter 17

Translated from Yiddish. These are the last two pages of a letter. The previous pages are missing. (M.A.)

Purim, March 22, 1905

if one can arrive sooner, then why not fulfill one's own wish, namely hindering oneself, because I don't see any other obstacles, and this way I will be able to see you once in two months, and even less does not matter to me, but I would like to know that you are near me. You don't have to think anything about Rokhl. She only meant my good, and the truth is all the same. If you were to send a ticket, then I would have more money, and, if not, this also does not matter to me. But the money is the same, because I spoke about this at home. So my father said to me: "For me it is all the same. If he sends you a ship's ticket, then I will give you 100 rubles for her." But in truth, for me it is all the same one way of the other. But in my opinion if I will have to take money or something else, that is, sending it from there and taking it over there.

We have no news. We are all in the best of health. May God grant that we hear the same from you. When we receive a letter from your parents, I will write you.

Remain healthy and happy, as wishes you, your eternally devoted Yente.

My parents, and also the children, send their warm regards and expect frequent and good letters from you. Now I will go send this letter and from there directly to Meisel to hear the Megillah. It is already Purim.

Yesterday I also wrote you a letter, an answer to the letter which took three weeks. It came later than the photographs.

Remain healthy.

According to the Jewish Colonial Trust list of shareholders, there were several Meisels in Svisloch. In Russia it was not uncommon, or rude, to refer to people by only their surnames.

The Megillah is the Book of Esther, often written in the form of a scroll, and read aloud at Purim. Purim is a happy holiday and is often celebrated with lots of noise. During the Megillah reading, the congregation may use "groggers," wooden or metal ratcheted noisemakers, to drown out the wicked Haman's name, when it is read out loud. Cheers erupt when the names of the heroic Mordecai and Esther are read. Purim is also a holiday when gifts of food are exchanged.

Letter 18

Translated from Yiddish. (M.A.)

New York, April 2, 1905

Dear Yente!

I received your letter yesterday with much joy. It also makes me very happy that you have received my cards. I thank you for immediately giving Aunt Chaya a card. I sent you three of the pin photographs which I made.

Again concerning what you write me of Rokhl, I write you that I cannot travel to them because I usually have no time. If you were there, there would have to be time, but not now, and I also do not feel like writing to them. So I wait further. Perhaps they will write to me first. Again, what you write that you understand that I was troubled enough over the fact that I did not earn money, I write you that I was, in fact, troubled. Now I am a bit more calm, but still not entirely. Imagine my situation. As I understand your letter, you are planning to travel immediately after Passover. I am very happy with that, but not entirely, because you will not be able to be with me. You will have to be with Rokhl. Who knows if you will be comfortable there. Therefore I cannot advise you on this. But it is, after all, your sister, so you should know better than I. I cannot know, because I don't know them.

And you don't have to be disturbed about my parents. I get letters from them all the time. They still write me that they don't have your address. But now I think that they have surely written. Write me whether they have in fact written to you.

He is also concerned about her voyage on the ship and encourages her to travel second class, rather than third-class steerage, as he had traveled.

In 1905, the first day of Passover was April 20th and Chaim is writing in anticipation of the holiday. When he mentions that he thought of asking for his family to make bed linen for him (linens were not usually store-bought) he means that he realizes his letter will not arrive before Passover and will not allow sufficient time for the project to be completed before work is stopped for the holiday. He most likely remembers how busy the women are cleaning and preparing the house for the holiday, getting their separate Passover dishes and cooking utensils ready. He hopes that Yente will travel immediately after Passover, so there is no point in asking for linens that cannot be ready to ship with her things.

Chaim recalls that he met Yente at Passover in 1903, when he was working on the rail-road that was being built through Svisloch. He celebrated the holiday with her family because he was away from his own family home in Brest.

Also, write me when you plan to leave. You don't have to be troubled about the trip. God will help, and you will come over in peace. But see to it that you have an official pass, and travel second class on the ship, and you can carry the money with you. But you have to be careful. I also ask you that if my parents come to you and invite you to their home, do not refuse them, and travel there for a few days. You will bring me much pleasure by [doing] that.

I had thought to write home, for them to make bed linen for me, but now I think that I will not write, because now it is already Passover, and after Passover there will be no time. There is no further news. I am, thank God, healthy. May God grant to hear the same from you. Remain healthy and happy. Have a happy Passover. Passover is two years since our acquaintance. It is already time for us to recount this happily.

From me, your eternally beloved Chaim.

Regards also to your parents, and wish them also a happy Passover. Regards also to the children. Adieu.

An Engagement Contract, Tenaim

Two copies of Chaim and Yente's engagement contract (tenaim, literally "stipulations" or "conditions") were with the letters.[114] They are written in Hebrew and Aramaic,[115] in Rabbi Korman's handwriting and are a negotiation between Rabbi Benjamin Korman, representing his son Chaim, and Rabbi Solomon Yesersky, representing his daughter Yente.

An engagement ceremony was binding and could be annulled only by a formal divorce.[116] Engagement contracts are still used, but are now often signed just before signing the ketubah, making it unlikely that the engagement would be dissolved. The ketubah itself is a prenuptial agreement which must be signed and witnessed before the marriage ceremony may begin. Having a tenaim is not a requirement now before a marriage can take place.

The Korman-Yesersky tenaim is quite traditional and the document set out the terms of the marriage, including the date and location of the wedding ceremony, dowry and responsibilities of the bride and groom.

Although marriages were usually prearranged by the families, both young people had to give their full approval to the bond. You can find an example of this mutual agreement in Genesis 24:57, where the agents of both Laban and Abraham arranged for Rebecca to marry Isaac. Before the agreement was completed, Rebecca was asked for her consent.[117] In our family, Chaim has asked Yente to marry him, and she has agreed. A traditional contract also usually stated that the betrothed couple shall not run away nor conceal from each other anything with regard to their possessions; rather they should equally share authority over their possessions, in peace and tranquility.[118]

The tenaim ceremony that took place at Yente's home in Svisloch announced that the two families had come to an agreement on the marriage of their two children. At the ceremony, the tenaim document was read out loud, signed and witnessed by Yaakov Brody, a relative of the Yeserskys, and Nosn Meir Ulyensky, whom I cannot identify.

A piece of crockery was probably smashed to seal the deal, perhaps to make a noise to frighten away evil spirits. Typically the parents saved the pieces or they were made into jewelry for the bride's friends.[119]

And then, as was the tradition, the assembled group celebrated with food.

The Korman/Yesersky Engagement Contract, *Tenaim*

Translated from Hebrew and Aramaic. These documents are the *tenaim*, the engagement contract. There are a few minor differences in the word order and some of the abbreviations between versions 1 and 2, but they are basically the same document. I suppose they made two copies, one for the bride's family and the other for the groom's. Both *tenaim* are written in Binyomin Korman's handwriting. (M.A.)

The *tenaim*, handwritten by Rabbi Benjamin Korinman, signed by Yaakov Brody and Nosn Meir Ulensky. A translation follows on the next page.

To good fortune. May it arise and sprout like a watered garden. He shall agree to the union. And may it obtain favor from the good God. He who finds a wife finds good.

May He who says from the beginning the end, may He grant a good name and remainder, to these words of the conditions and alliance, that have been negotiated and stipulated to between these two sides, on one side the scholar, our teacher Rabbi Binyomin Korinman who represents his son the praiseworthy groom Mr. Chaim, may he live, and on the second side the scholar, our teacher Rabbi Shlomo Yesersky who represents his daughter the praiseworthy virgin Miss Yenta, may she live.

First of all, this very groom Mr. Chaim, the above-mentioned, will marry, to good fortune and in a good and auspicious hour, the virgin, the praiseworthy bride Miss Yenta, the above-mentioned, through marriage and betrothal [chuppah ve-kiddushin] according to the laws of Moses and Israel, and they shall not run away nor conceal from each other but shall rather have authority over their possessions equally as is the way of the world, and in asking her, she said yes.

This very scholar, our teacher Rabbi Shlomo Yesersky, the father of the above-mentioned bride obligated himself to give generously a dowry to his daughter the bride in the amount of six hundred rubles and also obligated himself to clothe his daughter the bride with clothes for the Sabbath and holidays and weekdays as is the custom among the wealthy and also linen and scarves and shawls and pillows and blankets, all as is the custom.

This very above-mentioned groom Mr. Chaim has obligated himself to clothe himself with clothes for Sabbath and holidays and weekdays as is the custom among the wealthy aside from what he has in the way of cash as is known to him.

The time of the wedding will be, to good fortune and in a good and an auspicious hour, God willing, on the first of the month of Elul this year in the city of Philadelphia in the home of the bride's uncle who lives there.

Penalty from the side that breaks to the side that upholds shall be half the dowry and the penalty shall not be dismissed, etc. and if on account of etc. it shall stand according to the complete and ancient regulation. Clergy and musicians as is the custom.

And agreement from the bride and from the groom's father and from the bride's father, above-mentioned upon everything written here and explained above by using an object legally fit for this purpose on the eve of Monday 27 Adar Sheni 5665 here in Svisloch in the home of the bride's father.

And everything is valid and confirmed.

Signed - Yaakov Brody
Signed - Nosn Meir Ulyensky

Solomon is giving Yente a dowry of 600 rubles, money which she will bring to the marriage. In the case of divorce, the dowry was returned to the wife. Dowry money was both a sign of prestige and a way for a young couple to establish their life together. In 1905, Yente's dowry would have been worth about $300 in America.

A newly-married woman was also obliged to bring a trousseau with her that included her personal wardrobe, as well as the linen and bedding for the new home. Yente had written to Chaim (Letter 3) that she and her mother were sewing together to prepare these items.

The marriage date is set: 1 Elul 5665 which was September 1, 1905.

The bride's uncle is Harris Brody, Miriam Yesersky's brother. He is married to the bride's sister Rose.

Letter 19

Translated from Hebrew. (M.A.)

The letter was written in Hebrew, which was not normally used outside of study or prayer. Yiddish was the daily language.

Shlomo Mesersky is Solomon Yesersky, Yente's father. L. Yesersky is Yente's brother Lazar.

The letter is not dated, but the message indicates that it was written after the tenaim *ceremony, and Solomon wishes Chaim a happy Passover holiday.*

    I too will not refrain from seeking the peace of the beloved of my heart, the honorable Mr. Chaim Korman.

    Having nothing of which to inform you, for, thank God, we are healthy and peaceful, my words at the moment will be few, to ask you to inform us, from time to time, on your situation and on all that concerns you. My wife and all of the members of my household send their best to you and wish you congratulations and a happy and kosher holiday.

    Your friend, who wishes the best for you and loves you,

Shlomo Mezersky

Translated from Russian: (M.A.)

   Esteemed Korman,

Congratulations on your engagement and so I wish you merry holidays.

Yours, L. Yesersky

Lazer Yesersky's Russian addition to his father's letter.

Letter 20

Translated from Hebrew (M.A.)

To the honor of my dear father-in-law, the enlightened, the famous and exalted, the honorable, our teacher and rabbi, Shlomo Yesersky.

First I have come to inform you that we are, thank God, alive and well. May the Lord grant that we may hear good tidings from you, Selah.

Second, I can inform you that I have received your letter, and I cannot describe to you the greatness of the joy of my heart when I read it, and from the depths of my heart I congratulate you that it may come about in an auspicious hour. But upon my joy is cast a cloud of sorrow and that is that it is not in my ability to be with you to rejoice together. But the fault of this is not in us, for it is from the Lord. But I hope, with God's help, that you will yet derive joy from us from afar, and also in this I will rejoice very much for from now on it is within my ability to write you letters all of the time which was my chief duty which I could not fulfill until now.

From me, your son, who wishes you a happy and kosher holiday, Chaim Korman. I send regards to my dear mother-in-law Mrs. Miriam, may she live.

Dear Mr. Eliezer Yesersky,

From the depth of my heart I thank you for the regards which I just received and I congratulate you and wish you a happy holiday, from me, your brother, who blesses you seven times a day. Chaim Korman

Chaim replies to Solomon's letter in Hebrew, in the same formal style seen in Benjamin's letters.

Chaim is finally able to write as a member of the family after the signing of the tenaim.

Selah is an ancient Hebrew word of unknown meaning and uncertain grammatical status that appears in some books of the Bible, and is often left untranslated in English editions.

Eliezer is Lazar Yesersky.

Letter 21

Translated from Yiddish. A piece is missing, hence all the blank spaces. The signature is missing, but it is Chaim's handwriting. (M.A.)

New York, April 6

Very dear and esteemed Yente!

I received your letter with much joy, and you can just imagine the delight that I get from your letters. I think that you have no less from mine.

Concerning that which you write to me that I had written to my parents to ask you first about dowry money, you write that you can first write to me, as they say. I am writing to you, my dear, that you did not understand me, what I meant by that. I simply meant that my parents might ask how much dowry is being given. They are, after all, of the old world and know that without dowry, you don't have anything. Therefore I wrote to them to speak to you first. Because what does it matter --- will say more, they will --- pleased.

I wrote all of this only because of them. But it does not interest me. It seems to me that you should already know me a little. I know quite well that your parents will give you what they can. And you would also want to take more if you knew that your parents could give it. And if, God forbid, not, it would not matter. You are so dear to me, believe me, that if I were well situated, I would not want you to

This letter was written on April 6, 1905, three days after the signing of the tenaim. *Chaim is still concerned about Yente's dowry, not knowing that the amount—600 rubles—had been decided and included in the engagement contract.*

take any money from your parents.

Also, that you make - that I did not tell you to buy a lot of ---, now, after your having written, I am convinced that you are right. It is, in fact, necessary. I see that you are more sensible than I.

Further, what you write about Rokhl, that I don't understand her, that I judge her badly, it is possible that I have judged her badly. You have to excuse me because I don't know her yet. Even now, I don1 know her, but now I --- you write me. And concerning a ship's ticket --- all depends on you. If you had written me to send, I would have sent [it] to you. --- how can it be said that I should not have waited for writing and have sent it on my own? When would this have been? If I were well situated, and could bring you directly to me, then I surely would have done that. But things are not yet that way with us, and I did not know at all whether you wanted to travel already. Therefore I waited for you to write. Another reason I wrote you in my previous letter and again I figured what is the need of all this. I should send [money] to you and afterwards you would have to use it to take yourself to America, and it is entirely not necessary. And you figured this way too, as though our thoughts were in agreement. May God make it always like that.

Also, about going to Rokhl, who should write first to whom. Say what you want, but I am not going - in that, and the truth is that I have not --- and perhaps I could leave --- simply a shame --- a few dollars to you. I can write you the complete truth. Of course, if you were there, it would not be expensive for me. But now that I am alone, as much as possible, I can save money, so I have to save, but not on food or other necessary things. And I intend to write everything to her, and thus I put off everything.

I can also write you that I like your idea about coming here. To tell the truth, I am already counting the days. But one has to have patience. Everything in its time. I believe that you surely had a letter from my parents, and perhaps you have already seen each other. The request which I asked of you in my previous letter, you will surely fulfill when you are at our home before your voyage. You should bring a warm shawl for yourself, a heavy one. Here it is expensive. I will write you about your trip in another letter. Also write me -- exactly when you plan to leave ---

Letter 22

New York, April 17, 1905

Very esteemed and dear Yente! Be well.

I received your letter and everyone's letter today. Imagine the delight that I had reading the letters. I wish you luck. May we live happily and may we be happy with each other. Also our parents.

I am very happy that you had a good time on the evening of the engagement. I am also happy that my parents were at Uncle Feivel's and that Uncle was at home. Also, you write that I should write to my aunt a little more than I had written in the previous letter, I will now surely not write that way because before I could not write any other way. Everything was still hidden. Though we ourselves were absolutely decided, it really wasn't decided because I could not speak freely to everyone. But now, my dear, everyone knows and I can now write what I want freely. And the same with you. Also now I know that we are bound together one to the other, forever, forever, and it makes me very, very happy.

Also you write that I have to write a letter to Rokhl with congratulations, I also think that I will write. Further, it pleases me that my father asked you to come to Brisk, and that you will be there. I ask you also to travel when --- .
Also write me the reason why you have already decided not to travel to America immediately after Passover.

It pleases me very much that on Saturday night you are going to invite everyone to your house. Please write me who will be there. Also write me who was at the engagement. I ask you to write me about everything, because you can imagine how it interests me to know everything. I am here in America, and my thoughts are with you.

I think that I will not be in New York for Passover. I have already received several invitations for Passover. I think that I will go to a cousin of mine in Newark, a small town near New York. It costs 15 cents to go there. I will surely have a good time there, but I will be missing something ...

The 1905 population of Newark was 2576.

Remain healthy and happy, from me, your eternally loving, who hopes to see you soon,

Chaim Korman.

Regards to your parents and congratulate them. May they have pride and joy from us. Regards to the children also. I thank Bashke for her --- I would like to write more, but I can't now. It is Passover eve and there is no time. Be healthy. Adieu …

Letter 23

Translated from Yiddish. (M.A.)

New York, April 30, 1905

Dear and esteemed Yente!

I have received your letter and read it with great delight. I am very happy that you have decided to go to Brisk to my parents. But you write that you must go to Bialystok to get ready to go to Brisk. I don't think it is necessary for you to have to sew things in order to travel. But perhaps you find it necessary. Do what you think best.

Now, you write that you do not understand why I am troubled because I earn so little. I, in fact, should not be troubled, because I see that there are many people who earn nothing. But one cannot be satisfied, because we see those who earn a whole lot and want even more, and especially one who used to earn a lot and now earns less can surely not be satisfied. But you have to have hope that things will get better, and I hope that God Almighty will help so that we will be happy.

On the first days of Passover I was at my cousin's in a town near New York. A business was offered to me there and that I should settle there, but I myself did not --- on that. I have enough money for the business, but I couldn't decide because for me it seems a shame to throw away my job now. I do not yet know the work entirely, and, as things are, I cannot go back to that work, because whatever I know I would forget in that time. Because of that, it remained for me to go on working, and when I know the work well, then business can be made, if it is possible.

So I am healthy, thank God. May God grant to hear the same from you. Further, now that May is beginning, you should go for a walk every day and enjoy yourself and don't be troubled by anything. That is all that I require. I also thank you for calming me by saying that I should not be troubled by the fact that I only earn a little.

Write me exactly when you are going to leave, also when you are going to be in Brisk, write me everything, my dear!

Remain healthy and happy, from me, your beloved always, who hopes to be with you soon in happiness, Chaim Korman.

Regards to the parents, also to the children, from the depths of my heart, and wish them all the best and expect from them also good ---, from me the same. Adieu.

I also ask you, in the name of my [female] cousin with whom I can stay, when you are in Bialystok or in Brisk, buy her a good --- shawl for 8 to 10 rubles, also a light kerchief, also a good one, of the current style, and whatever it costs she will pay you here with great thanks too. Also, buy yourself a --- shawl because you use it also.

Your dear Chaim.

Letter 24

Translated from Yiddish (M.A.)

Svislotsh, 12 May

Very dear and best friend, Mr. Chaim Korman.

From the beginning of our writing, I come to inform you that we are, thank God, healthy. May God grant that we hear the same from you. We thank you very, very much for your good heart, in that you do not forget to write letters to us.

Dear Friend Korman, when we received your card, we were so happy as though we would have received from our own child. We ask you that when you receive our card to answer us immediately and to write how things are going with you in regard to livelihood and also about your health and to write whether your future bride has come to you.

Now we can write you that the first year has gone out to Kherson before Passover, and this week they left for the Far East. And also before Passover they took a thousand men from the division. From our fold, 19 men left on the first night of Passover, aside from the first year, all to the east.

We ask that it not grieve you that we did not send you an answer. There was no one to write the address. From us, your best friends, who wish you all good,

Avrohom Tsitrovsky and Teybe Tsitrovsky.

We request an answer.

Also, Peysach Altoske sends you his very friendly regards. I will send you a letter, but I am grieved because you do not want to write to me.

The Tsitrovskys are sending news about Chaim's former fellow soldiers. First they are sent to Kherson, a city in the Ukraine, 270 miles SSE of Kiev, and from there, they are sent to fight in the Russo-Japanese War in Manchuria.

There are two letters here; the last lines are from Peysach Altoske.

Letter 25

Translated from Hebrew. The signature at the bottom is not clear, but from the handwriting and content it is clear that the author is Binyomin Korman. (M.A.)

With the help of the Lord Almighty, Sunday of the Torah portion Behar, 9 Iyar 5665, Brisk

Peace and all goodness to my dear son Mr. Chaim, may he live.

I received your letter on the past holy Sabbath and I called the Sabbath a delight for how much was my soul sated with delight and pleasures on my seeing the writings of your hands and that you did inform me of your kind regards.

And with full heart I do send regards to my kinsman the brother of Yudl and all of his household, may they live, in that they did receive you in their home on the past Passover holiday. His brother Yudl was in my house before last Passover and related to me all of his situation and that he received a ship's ticket from his brother to travel to America, but he still is straddling the fence. And surely when

The secular date is May 14, 1905.

he decides in his mind to travel, he will be in my house before his departure.

Your brother Yechezkel is at the moment in the holy congregation of Zhmerinke at my brother-in-law Leyzer Goldfarb's, and his wages are not yet known. My brothers Yoel and Volf traveled last week to Vologda.

From my mechuten [son's father-in-law] I received a letter that he does not yet know the time of the departure of the bride, and when the time is fixed he will then certainly let me know beforehand in order to welcome her in happiness and to receive pleasure and delight for a short time before her departure.

From my sister Leah, may she live, I received a letter saying that you have written her that she should go to Brisk when the bride will be here to meet her face to face and to delight in her in love before her departure, and that she is prepared to fulfill your request. And in regard to your question, though time is hard pressed at the present, nevertheless "dismissed without anything is impossible," [the claimant should get some satisfaction] and surely I shall see to fulfill your desire within my ability and as is possible.

I also inform you that Noach the son of Yaakov Brubin, he too fled from the army and went to New York because most of our brethren from the regiments in Smolensk were sent to the war to the slaughterhouse ...

I also ask you to tell the orphan Chaye to write a letter to her mother for it has been an entire year that she has not heard a thing from her. I shall make an end to my words, I just send regards to my kinsman and friend Mr. Shimon Passman and his son Mr. Yosef and all his household, and to my kinsman and friend Mr. Chaim Tsvi Passman and his son Mr. Kaddish and all his household.

The one who loves you and seeks your peace and requests your good, sitting and expecting your answer speedily.

These stamps and postmarks are on the back of the envelope containing Letter 26, mailed in Svisloch on May 18, 1905 and arriving in New York on June 10, 1905, at 9:00 P.M.

Letter 26

Translated from Yiddish. (M.A.)

Svislotsh, 18 May

Dear, dear Chaim!

I received your two letters today coming home from Brisk. I was not at home for three weeks. I was in Brisk for eight days. I had a very good time. Your dear parents gave me a present, a dozen yarns and also small chains. Also Aunt Pesse gave me a ring.

I am going to America a few days after Shevues. I am going with a cousin of yours who was in New York, Hershl Sidelnik. He is getting a governor's pass, and he is taking me as a wife. He has already seen to making the pass, and when he is ready, we will leave immediately. But I will travel through Brisk.

Now I am writing letters to everyone in Brisk. Also to Kovel to my aunt. She traveled together with me from Brisk. Tsipe Tsiril's, your cousin, wants to go to America.

I already have everything ready for the trip. I am traveling, thank God, like a housewife. I have everything for the household, everything that is required for a household. May God allow us to use it in contentment. I would write you more but I am rushing to the post office. The mail is leaving soon, and I have to put in the letters to Brisk and to Kovel. I want them to go out today. Now write letters to my father's address, because probably no answers will reach me. I will travel to America, but I do not know the definite details of the trip.

Remain healthy and happy.

Yours, Yente.

Rokhl writes that I should leave as soon as possible. Now is a good time. Write an answer right away. Perhaps I will be in Svisloch. I will be concerned if there is no letter. I think that you won't be able to read what I have written, but forgive me because I am very rushed. Yours, Yente.

Everyone sends their warm regards.

Shevues (Shavuot) celebrates the harvest and commemorates the giving of the Ten Commandments to the Jewish People on Mt. Sinai. On Shavuot, Jews light candles, decorate with greenery, eat dairy foods, study Torah, attend prayer services, and read the Book of Ruth.

A governor's pass is a travel passport issued by the governor of a gubernia, which is like a state or province. Brest and Svisloch are in Grodno Gubernia.

Kovel is in the Ukraine, 250 miles WNW of Kiev. Chaim had worked on the construction of the Kiev-Kovel Railroad that opened in 1902.

Letter 27 is a postcard. This is the original one written by Yente.

Letter 27

Translated from Yiddish (M.A.)

Svisloch. 23 May

Esteemed Chaim!

Received your letter yesterday. I wonder why you did not receive my letter. I have written you very often lately. I think you have received my letters by now. Tomorrow I am sending out the baggage, and when Sidelnik writes me that the pass is ready, we will leave.

Remain healthy, from me Yente Yesersky.

My parents and the children send their warm regards.

Letter 28

Translated from Hebrew (M.A.)

The secular date is June 16, 1905.

With the help of the Lord Almighty. Friday. eve of the Holy Sabbath of the Torah portion Naso, 13 Sivan 5665, Brisk in Lithuania

Peace and all goodness to my dear son Mr. Chaim, may he live.

Before all discussion, I will inform you that we are all thank God alive and peaceful. I received your letter yesterday, and you do not have to worry and be troubled and be grieved in your soul that you have been exiled from the land of Russia and from the city of your birth and from the house of your father and your family to a distant and strange land, and to consider yourself alone and forlorn (lonely) for you have nothing to miss or to regret from what is heard now, the devastations and horrors in all of the land of Russia, pogroms and pillaging and in general the Jews in Russia are in an awful situation, may the Lord have mercy on them.

And also here in Brisk this week there was a big pogrom in some streets, and they looted and plundered much and also some people were killed by the guns and also many were wounded, because of the reserves, the rioters who came here by the thousands, and though at the moment the noise and tumult has quieted down, thank God, nevertheless, the city is in fear, may the Lord have mercy, and almost half the people have left the city.

There was a pogrom in Brest on the night of May 29, 1905. The city, a transit stop and army base for soldiers returning from the disastrous Russo-Japanese War, erupted in violence against ordinary citizens. This pogrom was instigated by drunken reservists.

And in truth, I will say that I envy those people who are in America. And if only I could find a buyer for my house, at its actual value, then I myself would also leave the land of Russia.

And concerning the yahrzeit, I inform you that it is the 16th of the month of Tammuz, that is, the 15th in the evening before the 16th.

In Judaism, a yahrzeit is the anniversary of someone's death, commemorated by near relatives with the lighting of a memorial candle and the reciting of Kaddish, the ancient prayer of mourning.

From my mechuten and the bride I receive many letters. And do inform me if she is writing to you at another address. I also inform you that the bride was in my house for eight days. We all of us seek your good peace and for God's sake answer immediately of all things concerning you.

Your father, who seeks your peace and expects your answer and your salvation.

Binyomin Korinman.

Yechezkel is in Kons---- Goldfarb for the holiday of Shevues he was at home. And he has not yet been informed how much his wages will be.

Letter 29

Translated from Hebrew (M.A.)

Friday, Eve of the Holy Sabbath. June 17/30 1905. Svislots
To the honorable, enlightened and esteemed Mr. Chaim Korman, may his candle shine.

The secular date is June 30, 1905.

Behold I am here to inform you that my gentle daughter Yente, may she live, went yesterday, Sunday of the week of the Torah portion Shlach, 16/29 June to your town, to your parents' house and from there will travel, if the Lord wills it. --- --- with Mr. Sudelnik to her desired destination. to America. You will surely also receive our letter from my daughter, may she live, from her trip. We are, thank God, all of us alive and well, and we seek your good peace and await your letter informing us of your condition and of all that concerns you, with impatience, from the one who blesses you with life and peace, blessings and success, who honors you and values you.

Shlomo Yesersky

Letter 30

Translated from Hebrew (M.A.)

The secular date is June 30, 1905.

Benjamin writes that Yente, the bride, will travel with Tsvi Sidelnik (another of Hersh Sidelnik's names).

Blessed is the Lord, Friday, the Eve of the Holy Sabbath of the Torah portion Shlach, 27 Sivan 5665, Brisk

Peace and all good to my dear son Mr. Chaim, may he live. And thank God that life and peace are with us, may God grant this for the days to come.

Behold yesterday the bride, may she live, came to my house and we received her with plenteous joy, and if God wills it on Sunday of the Torah portion Korach at evening she will be ready to travel for blessing to New York in an auspicious hour, with our kinsman Tsvi Sidelnik, may his candle shine.

May the Lord grant that they arrive in peace, and with all goodness may you be blessed from the Source of blessings and with the dew of success in all matters according to your desire and the desire of your father who seeks your peace and requests goodness for you, sitting and expecting your answer and waiting for your salvation and for the salvation of all Israel, and in truth I am surprised at you that you have withheld from me the fruit of your pen, not as before, therefore for God's sake write me immediately, clearly, a letter of greeting.

There is no more news. God willing it is still early. From me, your father, who seeks your peace,

Binyomin Korinman

The Grosser Kurfurst, The North German Lloyd Line, sailed from Bremen to New York City.

Yente Yesersky and Hersch Sidelnik sailed from Bremen on July 8, 1905 on The Grosser Kurfurst. They arrived at New York on July 18, 1905. The ship's manifest shows her name has been spelled "Jente Jezierska," lists her as age 22, and that she is from Svislocs, Russia. Yente lists her occupation as tailor, and that she is going to her uncle Harris Brody on Castor Road, Frankford, Philadelphia. Hersch Sidelnik is 33, a shoemaker from Brest Litowsk, and is going to New York.

Letter 31

Translated from Hebrew. (M.A.)

With the help of the Lord Almighty, Sunday, of the week of the Torah portion Shoftim, 26 Menachem (Av) 5665, Brisk in Lithuania

The secular date is August 27, 1905.

Peace and all goodness to my dear son, the darling of my heart, our teacher, Rabbi Chaim, may he live, with the peace of your wife, the refined, the highly esteemed Mrs. Yenta., may she live, with your uncle and father-in-law and your sister and all who accompany them and who are sheltered in their shadow, may they all be blessed with good lives and peace and all good, Selah.

Chaim is not a rabbi. Benjamin uses that title as a term of respect. Benjamin, on the other hand, is an ordained rabbi.

Behold I have received your letters one the eve of the holy Sabbath, at the time of the entrance of the Sabbath, and how we all did rejoice at the good tiding which came to us, that the day of your marriage and chief joy has already occurred this past Tuesday, 21 Menachem Av, for good fortune and in an auspicious hour, and from afar behold I do send you my threefold blessing which springs from the depths of my heart. Mazel tov, mazel tov, mazel tov.

Wedding was August 22, not as stipulated in engagement contract.

May the Lord grant you to rise higher and higher above the many blessings and successes and that your days and years be complete with goodness and fine things, with long life and prosperity and happiness and honor and all good in all matters. But, for God's sake, go in the way of the Torah and in the Jewish custom as is within your ability, and then my heart shall rejoice.

From lack of time I have made short at the present, and God willing in the days to come I shall send you a long letter. You shall also surely write me of the way the wedding took place there in order that I get pride and pleasure.

Behold I also seek the peace of Mr. Ziske Weinstein, and send me his address and also the names of all of your family there.

From me, your father Binyomin Korinman.

Letter 32

Translated ftom Yiddish. These are numbered pages five and six, and both pages are missing their last lines on my copy. On the second line there is a word "osmuraen" which is neither Yiddish nor Russian. Based on the time this letter was written (I assume it was at the same time as the others) and the mention of Harbin, it was probably at the time of the Russo-Japanese War, so it could mean "samurai." (M.A.)

This letter is not dated. I have placed it in this position because the writer knows that Chaim and Yente have married and drinks a toast to them.

Now the soldiers are rebelling in Russia. They are joining the "People's Freedom." One day the samurai go, and the soldiers the next.

We were in Harbin for one month. Then came a telegram saying that we should return. And that is what happened. It took 35 days for us to return to Smolensk, because the road was damaged, and the telegraphers were rebelling. So we

A previous letter from the Tsitrovskys and Peysach Altoske was written from Svisloch.

Russian Guards on review.

Smolensk was outside the Pale of Settlement where the majority of Jews lived. Michael Hickey, in Acta Slavica Iaponica, *has written that, despite the location, there was a sizeable self-sustaining Jewish population in Smolensk. He noted that there were prayer houses, Jewish schools, kosher butcher shops, and other necessities for a Jewish community. Hickey wrote that the first pogrom in Smolensk occurred on July 24, 1905. It was perpetrated by rioting soldiers and dozens of Jewish shops were destroyed.*

had to remain on the road for several days. On my arrival in Smolensk, I went into Tsitrovsky. He told me that he had received a letter from you. I immediately began to read it and for great joy kissed [it/him?], because I never believed that I would remain alive and come back to Smolensk and read your letter ... [The dots are in the original.]

Now I can congratulate you. May God grant good fortune to you and the same for your wife. Write me whether she is the one you told me about when you were still in Smolensk. Tonight I am drinking a toast at Tsitrovsky's for you and for your wife and for all Israel. Write me in what month is ---

Now I send regards to you and to your friends also. I ask you not to refuse me, and send me an answer immediately. And you should write everything to me, what is happening with you in America. And first of all, how you are doing with a livelihood. And what has happened to you until now ...

From me, your best friend, Peysekh Altoske

And Avrohom and Teybe Tsitrovsky send you their regards too. They wish you and your wife good fortune. They thank you very much for your letters. You simply delight them.

They wanted to nail Tsitrovsky's store shut, but things quieted down. He only suffered fear. There was also a pogrom in Smolensk. And Avrohom and Teybe request an answer. They asked me to write a separate letter for you, but time has led me to write a new one.

I ask you to write me a letter at Tsitrovsky's address, but you should write a separate one.

Remain healthy and live happily, this is wished you by your best ---

Letter 33

The envelope for this letter is postmarked 24 October 1905 New York. This letter, as well as the following letter, seem to be from Joe Passman, Chaim's cousin in New York.

October 23, 1905

To our dear (male and female) cousins Korman,

Be advised that we are, thank God, healthy. May God grant that we hear the same from you. We received your postcard. Excuse us for not answering you, because when I want to write, my son does not permit me. This is the absolute truth. If you do not want to believe me, you will be convinced next year yourselves.

Now I ask you to write me whether you have received an answer from the old country about Peskin. I can report to you that Yidl Zigman went home one day after Rosh Hashanah, and I sent a greeting with him for your sake, and I am expecting an answer soon.

We send you regards from the depths of our heart and we ask you to answer soon.

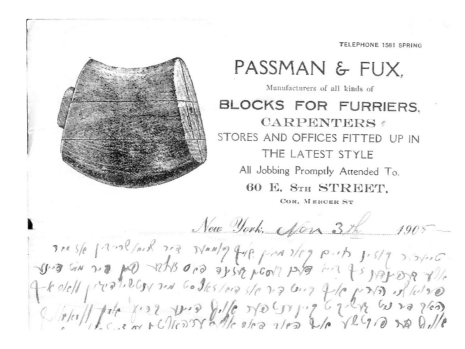

TELEPHONE 1581 SPRING

PASSMAN & FUX,

Manufacturers of all kinds of

BLOCKS FOR FURRIERS,

CARPENTERS

STORES AND OFFICES FITTED UP IN
THE LATEST STYLE

All Jobbing Promptly Attended To.

60 E. 8TH STREET,

COR. MERCER ST

New York, Nov 3rd 1905

Left: This letter is written by Joseph Passman, the cousin with whom Chaim lived when he arrived in New York in 1904. His letterhead shows a unique combination of business specialties; they manufactured wooden blocks for furriers as well as carpentry for office and store interiors. The 1906 New York City Directory shows that Joe was working at Passman and Fux, furriers at 125 E. 4th Street and living at 92 E. 4th St. A postcard from Brest that arrived in New York on June 28, 1905 was forwarded to 60 E. 8th Street.

The 1907–1908 NYC Directory no longer lists Passman and Fux furriers; they have become Passman and Fux carpenters at 60 E. 8th St. and Joe continues to live at 92 E. 4th St. This emphasis on carpentry explains his remarks that he works "inside and out."

Letter 34

Nov 3, 1905

Dear Cousin Chaim Korman,

I write you that we are all in the best of health. May we hear the same from you and your wife. I ask you to forgive me for not sending you an answer to your letters and also to the picture. I received it all. It seems that you have not received my two letters.

Your picture, when I received it, I immediately gave it out to a picture maker, and he told me that at most it would take two weeks. [Another] takes much longer.

The reason is that I am very busy. I have much work inside and outside, and we now work hard. I am very happy that you are in the best of health and also that you are earning good wages. I wish you success in your work, that you should be able to work your way up quickly and be independent in business.

Concerning Hersh, I cannot write you any good news. He caused the match with Brayne to be abandoned, and he will travel away with her to a country and live like husband and wife. He writes letters home that he is not healthy and that he cannot work. To the contrary, he is healthy like and he earns up to 15 a week. Chaim Hersh's address is 234 E. 3 Street.

No more to write. Remain healthy and happy.
Your devoted Joe Passman.

Regards to your dear wife. Regards to Mr. Klein, Mrs. Broida (Brody). Our whole family sends warm regards to you and your wife.

Chaim and Yente may have had photographs taken in Philadelphia and then sent to Joe in New York to be made into the large portraits that were found with the letters. These photos were inscribed with greetings from Joseph Passman.

I cannot identify Hershel or Brayne.

He calls Rose, "Mrs. Broida," another version of Brody. I do not know who Mr. Klein is.

Letter 35

Translated from Yiddish. The dots (...) are in the original. The dashes (---) are in place of words in the original that I could not decipher. (M.A.)

I cannot identify Freyde, the woman who wrote this letter. She may be a relative; she is certainly close to Yente.

The distance between Svisloch and Warsaw is about 135 miles.

From the beginning of 1905, following Bloody Sunday in St. Petersburg when the Army fired on a peaceful crowd coming to petition the Czar for reforms, Russia was beset with a series of strikes. The railroad workers' strike in October paralyzed the entire country and led to the Czar's October Manifesto, which promised concessions.

Svisloch, 4 November 1905

Dear, dear Yenteshe, darling!

I am ashamed to write to you after not having written you for so long. I will write you the reason, and you yourself will understand that I am not guilty, but rather the times made it so that I had to forget about you a little, my dear! Not for a long time.

Our Dinah was not healthy. She was sick with typhus. She is now in Warsaw, that is, she works in Warsaw, so I went to her directly and had to sit next to her. You can imagine my grief sitting in Warsaw, confused. She was sick for four weeks. Now she is better. I brought her to me to recuperate last week. Now in Warsaw typhus (starving typhus) is raging. Since the trains have been on strike, a great mass of people have suffered hunger, and many have died from hunger, and the remainder suffer from typhus, and of course such a disease is contagious. It also did not miss us.

Now they say that the trains will again be stopped, and for the workers it is very, very difficult. More correctly, they are stuck. I was in Warsaw, so I heard from workers. They say when the trains stop, all workers must dig a pit and throw themselves in alive. In one word, it is now in general in Russia a bad time, ready to burst [?]. I don't find it necessary to write you about Russia. I know very well that you read the newspapers as I do. But you, Yente and Chaim have to be pleased that you are now in America. At this time, there are many people who are jealous of the people who are not now in Russia.

Now Yentele I can write you about your parents. Yesterday I was at their house and asked about everything, and I have to write to you. First because I want to write to you and second because I in fact want to be --- because you ask me, so I can write you that they are healthy. Your dear father drinks hot water because he says that he wants to fulfill your order, and he feels a lot better. And mainly Yenteshe they get delight from you, that things are good for you and are happy to have delight from their children. And further at home everything is the same as you have read. They all look very good. I have written you everything about your household.

I entirely forgot, you ask about me? And how I live? It is wonderful for me that you should forget Svisloch life so quickly. But if you would forget about our life it would please me very much. Surely American life has made you forget our life. No! I will not write to you. Then you should be able to --- and see that our life is no good. It is better for you not to know because if you did know you would say it is a pity for us.

But I do write to you and ask that if you want to give delight to me you should write me frequent letters and that is for me the biggest delight. You cannot imagine my delight when I receive a letter from you. I read it over several times and keep getting more delight that things are so good for you, and I want to see you very much and have a good time with you together. But unfortunately we must be so far apart. In truth I did not imagine that I would miss you so much. Believe me that with whomever I speak and whoever comes to me, it seems to me that it is no one else but Yente.

Yet I now have many acquaintances. We have in Svisloch female teachers, educated young women, graduates of the gymnasia, they come in to us and request my company, and they bring me a --- So everything is as it was. I live as I have in Svisloch. Of Svisloch I can write you who got married and who has gotten engaged. Beylke Libnen got engaged to Menachem Rubin. The wedding will be soon. How do you like that match? And Levintsig got married. But I cannot write you about his wife's qualities, educated, perfect Russian and also Hebrew and also a --- beauty. I met her just yesterday evening. I was at Tsoylan's visiting and she was there but she made a very good impression on me. When I was told about her, I didn't believe everything, that someone with so many qualities would marry the foolish Mendl. Yes, I saw for myself that it is true. It is the money that does this ... Now she has looked around and sees that he also does not have any money, but she has remained with Mendl ...

Nice, I have written you about all of the nonsense because by my nature I hate writing about other people. Usually when I write, I write about my own interests. Now dear Yenteshe, I received your photograph. I thank you very much for sending it to me by which you made me very happy. When I saw the photograph I wanted to ask you why you are so serious and you don't want to give me a smile. And I very much wanted to give Chaim a pinch in the nose so much did his face express to me. In a word, you look very good and I am pleased with your card. I know everything about you Yente ... Your father told me everything. He tells me that you write about Rokhl and Rokhl writes about you. Meanwhile we know all --- about you. Write me Yente more often, and write whether you have received my letters. I am in doubt if you have received my letters, because I have not yet had an answer to my letters from you. Now I will write you the address to which you wrote me. I will continue to write to you but I am --- from writing. I don't have any patience. You can already tell from my writing that I am writing without patience. So I am ending my writing with the hope that you will write me a little more often and from my side there will never be a ---.

Greetings and kisses to you.

Your ever not forgotten, Freyde ---

Very friendly regards to your --- If he writes me, I will write back. If not, then I won't write to him.

The above.

Born in Palestine in 1917, Ygael Gluckstein became a Marxist in the 1930s. He moved to England in the 1950s and changed his name to Tony Cliff. He founded the group that became the Socialist Workers Party. He wrote this view of the strikes, from a worker's stance, published in the Socialist Worker Review:

"Finally, on 6 August, the Tsar made a concession. But instead of giving the long promised National Assembly, nothing was given but a consultative body—the Duma—with no power to legislate. The Duma was at the mercy of the Tsar. Out of the 1,400,000 Petersburg citizens only 13,000 had the vote. This roused the popular passion to fever heat, and led to the second great wave of strikes in October, in which the demands were overwhelmingly political.

At the same time the demand for the eighthour day was central. The strike started in Moscow and from there it spread to Petersburg. The Petersburg soviet was established. By 13 October the number of strikers throughout Russia exceeded one million. Practically all the railway lines were stopped. The post stopped, schools were closed, water and gas supplies ceased, the country, the cities and the communications between them were practically at a standstill. Poland was completely paralyzed by the strike, as was Finland."

Letter 36

Translated from Yiddish. The greeting and signoff are translated from Hebrew. (M.A.)

The secular date is September 11, 1906.

Yente gave birth to their first child, Max William Korman, on July 10, 1906. His Hebrew name was Mordecai, in memory of Benjamin's father.

The pidyon haben is the ancient ceremony to redeem the firstborn son from the priesthood. This redemption ceremony is mentioned in Exodus, Numbers, and Leviticus. A minyan is required for the ceremony, which takes place one month after the child's birth, and there is a payment of five pieces of silver to the Kohen. This payment is often returned as a gift to the child. It is a happy occasion and celebrated with friends. There are many restrictions on the suitability of the child, and only about 1 in 10 qualifies. It must be a first male child; it cannot be a caesarean delivery; the mother may not have had a previous miscarriage or abortion; and the parents may not be Levites. Not qualifying is not detrimental to the child or his family in any way.

The bris is the circumcision ceremony performed on the eighth day after the birth of a male child.

Samuel Korman was born to Chaya and Yechezkel on September 5, 1906.

With the help of God Almighty

Thursday, in the week of the Torah portion Tavo, 16 Elul 5666, Brisk

To my dear son, the beloved of my heart, the young gentleman, Mr. Chaim Korman, may his candle shine, with his refined and modest wife, Mrs. Yente, may she live. May you be written and sealed immediately in the book of the righteous and the just for good, long lives, and for peace and all good things, Amen, Selah.

First of all, I write that we here are all, thank God, healthy, and concerning the tribulations that are happening in Russia in the big cities, among us in Brisk it is, thank God, quiet. May God grant further that it be quiet in all of Russia and that we hear, one from another, good tidings from afar.

Secondly, I write that I received your card today, and I absolutely do not understand when you write that you are very concerned that you have not had any letters from us for such a long time. It seems to me that in the meantime I have already sent you three letters. This is the fourth.

Also, you did not send regards from your wife Yente, may she live, and of how the child is. You also did not write about the Pidyon Haben, when it was. I also write that last week a card arrived from you which you wrote on the day after the 17th of Tammuz, the day that she gave birth to the boy with good fortune, and the card that you wrote on the day following the bris arrived here four weeks later, on the 15th of Av. This surprises me that it should be delayed for so long. Probably my letters which I wrote you were also delayed. I suppose that in the meantime my letters reached you. Therefore you should immediately write an answer to me to this letter, and you should, for God's sake, write me about everything. There is no more news to write in the meantime. From me, your father, who seeks your peace, and wishes for your good, and expects your answer and awaits your salvation and the salvation of all Israel.

Binyomin Korinman

After the earlier writing, news arrived delaying the letter a few hours. I send you congratulations. Chaya, Yechezkel's wife, had a male son.

And they lived happily ever after …

I started writing this book to help my family understand the 36 letters by recreating their context. I never meant to write an extensive family history, but I think there's a need to explain a bit more in order to fill in some of the gap between their immigrant housing in South Philadelphia and Sunday dinners at the country club.

Settled in Philadelphia, Chaim, now Hyman, continued to work in the garment trade. He supported his wife Yetta and son Max and sent one of the six dollars he earned each week back to his father in Russia.[120] According to Leonard Korman's autobiography, Hyman enrolled in the old Central High School to learn English while he worked in a factory manufacturing ladies suits and dresses. He started as office boy and general assistant, a job that included sweeping the floors before and after work. The 1908 Philadelphia City Directory shows him living in a row house at 628 Tasker Street in South Philadelphia, and describes his occupation as "clothctr." The 1910 City Directory shows him living at the same address

Central High School for Boys, located at Broad and Green Streets, 1900. *King's Views of Philadelphia.*

Hyman asked Jake Smigelski to join him in a garbage-hauling business. Jake was married to Gittle, Miriam and Harris's younger sister, who was closer in age to her niece Yetta. Jake had arrived in Philadelphia in 1906, and Gittle followed with their children in 1907. Jake's granddaughter Janis Samuels Quaile remembers hearing this story and notes that Jake declined Hyman's offer, choosing to remain a farmer.

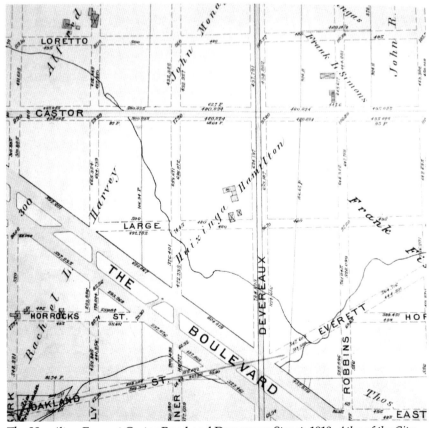

The Hamilton Farm at Castor Road and Devereaux Street, 1910. *Atlas of the City of Philadelphia.*

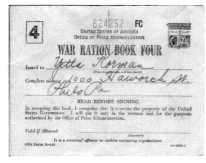

Hyman Korman's World War I Registration Card, front. He is a self-employed farmer on Castor Road. Yetta's name has been listed in error as Henrietta. His birth date is shown as 1880.

August was "polio season" and many people were afraid to go to crowded places, such as swimming pools and theaters. Polio was communicable and could be deadly. Its other name was infantile paralysis, and it left many children and young adults unable to breathe or walk normally.

Yetta Korman's World War II ration book. Their home is 1000 Haworth Street at the corner of Castor Avenue.

but lists him as "foreman." In his years at the factory he rose to General Superintendent in charge of all production.

The 1910 US Federal Census shows that the Kormans, including sons Max and Sam, still lived on Tasker Street but soon after, Hyman rented the Hamilton Farm at Castor Road and Devereaux Street. The family moved to the Oxford Circle neighborhood and Hyman continued to work in the clothing factory in center city; he hired a farmer to help him. Farming was an essential service during World War I; Hyman was not eager to be sent back to Europe as a soldier, and farmers were not conscripted. In 1917, he purchased the farm, his first land acquisition. The 1920 census shows Hyman still farming on Castor Road. Peter Cherin, a fellow Russian immigrant described as a farm laborer, lived with them.

Yetta cared for her family, worked on the farm and also took in boarders to supplement their income, and they made some life-long friends in this way. Families would come to escape summer in the inner-city as those were the days before air-conditioning, and the control of polio was still a distant dream. I can only begin to imagine the patience and diplomacy necessary to share one's kitchen with another family. Sarah was born on the farm in 1916 and remained friendly with the children of some of the boarders; many of these children had been enlisted to keep her, the baby, amused.

Hyman's brother, Yechezkel, arrived in 1913 to begin a life in America, intending to send for send for his wife Chaya and the children; upheaval in Rus-

Loading gravel, 1937. *New York Public Library.*

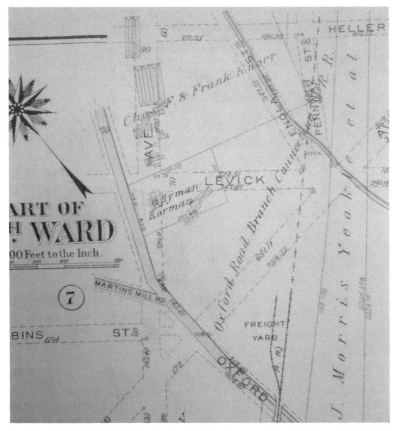

Hyman Korman's property on Oxford Avenue at Levick Street, 1921.
Atlas of the City of Philadelphia.

Hyman Korman, on his tractor, 1930s.

Max and Sarah Korman, mid-1920s.

sia and WW I prevented them from emigrating until 1921. Yechezkel "became" Oscar and lived with Hyman and Yetta and, like his brother, Hyman, learned a trade in the garment industry. Oscar's 1917 WWI Draft Registration shows he was employed as a coat presser at Kirschbaum and Company at Broad and Washington Streets in South Philadelphia, and the 1920 Federal Census places him at 139 Reed Street as a boarder. Benjamin had died in Brest in 1919 and Hudel accompanied her daughter-in-law and grandchildren on the journey to Philadelphia. Upon their arrival, Oscar settled with his wife, now "Ida," and family at 409 Cross Street in South Philadelphia where they lived for the rest of his life.

When they arrived in America, Chaim and Yente transformed themselves into Hyman and Yetta. A name change was the first step most took to shed their "greenhorn" identity. Family life took them to a new American level; they became "Mom" and "Pop" to their children. Until his death, many of his friends referred to Hyman as "Pop Korman" but to his children, grandchildren and great-grandchildren, he is always "Pop."

Leonard Korman wrote:

My father told me how one Sunday morning there was a great family conference. My grandfather had decided that the time was right for him to

Lawndale Apartments, 6700-08 Oakley Street. The land was purchased in 1925 and 1926 and construction begun soon after. *Photograph courtesy of Diane Casey.*

The 1200 block of Levick Street, typical of Northeast Philadelphia postwar style row houses, typically 1500-1800 sq. ft. on two floors. *Photograph courtesy of Diane Casey.*

Oxford Court, the garden court apartment where Hyman lived with Sarah after Yetta's death.

Sarah was hired as a receptionist in the moveable office. One day a tenant called to complain that he had no heat while Mr. Korman was "warming his tootsies" down in Florida. My mother was furious that someone would speak rudely about her father, and spoke her mind. Her father fired her. Her mother's reaction was, "Good, now we can go shopping!"

give up his job as Plant Manager … I am told that my grandmother objected strongly to this idea. She mentioned that he had toiled all these years and was now quite secure economically. But her objection could not change my grandfather's mind.

The Kormans purchased and moved to another farm on Oxford Avenue in the Lawndale neighborhood, not far from the farms where Yetta's brothers Isaac and Samuel were raising their families. Hyman continued to buy farm land and in 1921 decided that the time was right to begin building homes.

Hyman had worked in the building business in Russia but not for himself; he worked in the S.I. Bak & D.K. Raskin Office of Civil Buildings in Sarny, building the Kiev-Kovel railroad. He and his uncles Velvyl and Yoyl Korinman built the housing for the people who were in the field building the railroad. Now he was prepared to use that experience in Philadelphia, and he started by building single homes, one or two at a time. The office was a moveable building on skids and they used a tractor to pull it from job to job.[121]

The business picked up when Max joined the venture in 1924, and Sam in 1928. Both studied architecture in night classes at Drexel Institute, and the Kormans became developers of whole neighborhoods of homes, apartments, and stores.

Hyman and Yetta had become naturalized Americans in 1911, but there were some aspects of a fearful shtetl childhood that couldn't be forgotten. Hyman never put the same birth date on any documents; many people truthfully did not know when they were born, but he was educated and certainly knew his true age. I think the real issue was his persistent worry that the Russian Army might be able to locate him. Yetta also remembered the bad times in Russia and didn't want her money tied up in a bank if she needed to flee. Berton Korman tells the story about how Yetta would bury cans of money in the dirt floor in the farmhouse basement. When the Frankford Trust Company asked Hyman to pay down his loan during the Depression, Yetta dug up her stash of money and was able to pay off the debts of her husband's business, and also those of a friend, and fellow builder.

It's difficult to say what makes a family close. In every decade of census records I can find clusters of the Yeserskys and Kormans living in the same area of the city. Yetta and her siblings socialized, and the children, the cousins of that generation, knew one another. It seemed that the entire family was invited to each bar mitzvah and wedding. Max and Sam Korman worked with their father in the family building business. During WWII, they went back to farming and three generations lived together on a farm in Newtown, PA where Sarah shared a room with her niece Lynne. In the late 1940s, Max, Sam, and Sarah built their new homes within a block of each other and their children attended the same schools. About 1960, Lynne, Bert, and Leonard moved to their first houses on the same block in Jenkintown. A decade later, the cousins bought a farm, divided it into building lots, and built homes for themselves. Barney Moss joined the business when he and Sarah married, and all of Max, Sam, and Sarah's sons joined as they graduated from college. Such closeness is extremely unusual in businesses and families.

Three photographs on left: Castor Avenue north of Oxford Circle was the center of Hyman Korman Inc.'s building in the 1940s. One of the forward-thinking features of these stores was having free parking on a large lot in the rear.

The window in the right-hand side of the top photograph is the Korman office. A sign in the window advertises Insurance and Apartments.

Castor Avenue was a shopping street for a large neighborhood of row houses and twin homes. It's interesting that all the people in the photographs are women and children. It was not unusual to see a baby carriage containing a sleeping child left alone on the sidewalk outside a store while the mother was shopping inside.

Advertisement for single homes, priced from $9500, and twins from $6250. The homes had three or four bedrooms, two baths, and a two-car garage.

Hyman Korman Builders office, 6401 Castor Avenue, Philadelphia, 1947.

Eventually Hyman Korman Inc. became one of the largest home builders in the northeast United States. Hyman was a founder of Temple Sholom Synagogue, where he built the Rabbi Benjamin Korman Memorial Chapel; the synagogue was located adjacent to his original Hamilton Farm. He was a member of Jewish country clubs and the Boy Scouts of America; he sat on boards as diverse as Federation of Jewish Agencies and the Cystic Fibrosis Foundation. The Korman Research Building is part of Einstein Medical Center in Philadelphia. The Jewish Theological Seminary of America honored him with The Louis B. Marshall

The Korman family at the dedication of the Rabbi Benjamin Korman Memorial Chapel, Temple Sholom Synagogue, Large Street and Roosevelt Boulevard, Philadelphia, 1952.

Front left: Judith Korman. Behind from left to right: Mae Silverman Korman, Hyman Korman, Max Wm. Korman, Berton Korman, Matilda Korman, Leonard Korman, Steven Korman, Lynne Korman, Samuel J. Korman, Bernice Korman, Sarah Moss, I. Barney Moss. Front right: Joan Moss.

Barney Moss, Sam and Bert Korman, 1938.

Award, which is presented to individuals who demonstrate the exemplary ethics and philanthropic commitment embodied by Louis Marshall, an esteemed constitutional lawyer and former board chair of JTS. Hyman was a trustee of Frankford Hospital and, from its inception in 1937, treasurer of the Home Builders Association of Philadelphia for 27 consecutive terms! Hyman always supported Jewish education, and the students at the Talmudical Yeshiva of Philadelphia attend the Hyman Korman High School, which the Yeshiva named in his memory at the time of his death.

Hyman and Yetta in Florida, 1940.

Yetta Korman's costume jewelry brooch, shown at its actual size.

While he had a special interest in Jewish education and charities, Hyman was truly ecumenical. He was a trustee of Nazareth Hospital, a Catholic institution, and the nuns, in appreciation, crocheted colorful afghan blankets for him. He became one of the first Jewish bankers in Philadelphia as a trustee of Frankford Trust Company, a bank with Quaker roots.

His grandsons remember seeing him sign stacks of checks, for large and small amounts, which were sent to the individuals and charities that approached him. He never refused a request for assistance. My father told me that he anonymously paid the rent for some storekeepers who fell behind.

I'd like to leave you with one wonderful Yiddish word: *"kvell."* It's from Middle High German *quellen*, to "gush" or "swell." It means to be extraordinarily proud and to rejoice. *Kvell* is what I do when I speak about our family.

Mom and Pop, Yetta and Hyman, became an American success story. Their marriage was a success; their business was a success (now into its fourth generation). They had a commitment to their community. Their family grew and multiplied.

Cover of the program book for the dedication of the Rabbi Benjamin Korman Memorial Chapel.

Pop and Mom

NOTES

1 Ashbourne Country Club, Cheltenham, PA.

2 "If I Were a Rich Man," from *Fiddler on the Roof*. A musical with music by Jerry Bock, lyrics by Sheldon Harnick, and book by Joseph Stein, set in Tsarist Russia in 1905.

3 JewishGen.org is a website for Jewish genealogy research, an independent nonprofit organization affiliated with the Museum of Jewish Heritage.

4 *"Shtetl"* is a Yiddish term for a town with a Jewish population. *"Shlep"* is from the German *schleppen*, to drag.

5 http//www.Jewishfamilyhistory.org.

6 The area in Western Russia where the Jews were allowed to live from 1792 until 1917.

7 Howe, *World of Our Fathers*, 7.

8 Ibid., 11.

9 Ibid., 13.

10 Ibid., 14.

11 Kriwaczek, *Yiddish Civilization*, 231.

12 Shandler, "Reading Sholem Aleichem from Left to Right."

13 "Pogrom" in *The Columbia Encyclopedia*, 2254.

14 Howe, *World of Our Fathers*, 11.

15 Spiro, "Crash Course in Jewish History."

16 "Pogrom" in *The Columbia Encyclopedia*, 2254.

17 Antin, *The Promised Land*.

18 Howe, *World of Our Fathers*, 10.

19 Ibid., 10.

20 Ibid., 9.

21 Gilbert. *Atlas of Jewish History*, 72.

22 Ibid., 72.

23 Spiro, "Crash Course in Jewish History," part 56.

24 "Brest-Litovsk," *The Encyclopedia Britannica*.1910,Vol. IV, 500.

25 "Brest City Overview," http://www.Brest-Belarus.org

26 *The Jewish Encyclopedia*, 1902.

27 Medvedevsky, "Brest, Belarus."

28 Kaplan, "The Jews of Brest in the 19th Century," 93.

29 Medvedevsky, "Brest, Belarus."

30 "Brest Fortress," http://www.belarusguide.com/cities/castles/BrestFortress.html.

31 Weisser, *A Brotherhood of Memory*, 57.

32 Ain, "Swislocz—Portrait of a Shtetl."

33 Weisser, *A Brotherhood of Memory*, 57.

34 Ain, "Swislocz—Portrait of a Shtetl."

35 Weisser, *A Brotherhood of Memory*, 57.

36 Ain, "Swislocz—Portrait of a Shtetl."

37 Weisser, *A Brotherhood of Memory*, 57.

38 Ain, "Swislocz—Portrait of a Shtetl."

39 Ibid.

40 Ibid.

41 Levykin, "Face to Face With the Czars." *St. Petersburg Times*

42 *The Columbia Encyclopedia*, 498.

43 Howe, *World of Our Fathers*.

44 *Columbia Encyclopedia* 2127.

45 Mann. "It Had Its History."

46 Feldbluym, *Russian-Jewish Given Names*, 42.

47 Mann, "It Had Its History."

48 Spiro, "Crash Course in Jewish History," part 57.

49 Feldbluym, *Russian-Jewish Given Names*, 42.

50 Kriwaczek, *Yiddish Civilization*, 277.

51 Spiro, "Crash Course in Jewish History," article 57.

52 Handler. "Revision Lists," http://www.jewishgen.org.

53 Mann. "It Had Its History."

54 Howe, *World of Our Fathers*, 7.

55 http://www.MyJewishLearning.com.

56 Spiro, "Crash Course in Jewish History," article 57.

57 "A Russian Jew's Story." *The New York Times*.

58 "Anti-Semitism." *Encyclopaedia Britannica*, Volume II, 139.

59 Aronson, " The Attitudes of Russian Officials in the 1880s Toward Jewish Assimilation and Emigration," 1.

60 Lilly, "The Russian Famine of 1891–92."

61 "Emigration 1881–1914: The Plight of Russian Jews." http://www.ballinstadt.de.

62 Levykin, "Face to Face with the Czars."

63 "Russo-Japanese War." *The Columbia Electronic Encyclopedia*.

64 Levykin, "Face to Face with the Czars."

65 Klier, *Pogroms: Anti-Jewish Violence in Modern Russian History*, 347

66 Spiro, "Crash Course in Jewish History," article 57.

67 Klier, *Pogroms: Anti-Jewish Violence in Modern Russian History*, 229.

68 Kaplan, "The Jews of Brest in the 19th Century."

69 Archangel Michael, "Antiochian Orthodox Christian Arch diocese."

70 Kaplan, "The Jews of Brest in the 19th Century."

71 Klier, *Pogroms: Anti-Jewish Violence in Modern Russian History*, 347.

72 Korman Letter 28.

73 Spiro "Crash Course in Jewish History," article 57.

74 Gilbert, *The Atlas of Jewish History*, map 76.

75 Ship's manifest.

76 "Women in Steerage," *New York Times*.

77 Howe, *World of Our Fathers*, 69.

78 Ibid., 97.

79 Korman Letter 10.

80 "Sweating System."*The Columbia Encyclopedia*, 2762.

81 White, "Cardiovascular and Tuberculosis Mortality: The Contrasting Effects of Changes in Two Causes of Death,"289.

82 Miller, "Philadelphia: Immigrant City."

83 Ibid.

84 Ibid.

85 Feldman, "The History of the Philadelphia Jewish Federation."

86 Boonin, "The Jewish Quarter of Philadelphia."

87 Miller, "Philadelphia: Immigrant City."

88 "Philadelphia City Hall," http://en.wikipedia.org/wiki/Philadelphia_City_Hall.

89 King, *Philadelphia and Notable Philadelphians.*

90 Southeastern Pennsylvania Transportation Authority. http://septa.org.

91 "Wanamaker's." http://en.wikipedia.org/wiki/John_Wanamaker_Store Beginnings.

92 Boorstin, Daniel J. *The Americans: The Democratic Experience.*

93 "Lit Brothers," http://www.Wikipedia.com.

94 "N. Snellenburg and Co.," http://www.Wikipedia.com.

95 Boorstin, Daniel J. *The Americans: The Democratic Experience.*

96 Deganith, "Rabbi Benjamin Korman," 417.

97 Berton Korman's recollection.

98 Yesersky Letter 6.

99 Sarah Moss's recollection.

100 Alsher, "Observations and English translation of Korman/ Yesersky Letters."

101 Korman Letter 1.

102 Korman Letter 1.

103 Korman Letter 12.

104 Harris Brody had a hay business at 749 S. 4th Street, *1898 Philadephia City Directory.*

105 Brody letterhead, Korman Letter 9.

106 1900 United States Federal Census.

107 S.S. Haverford, Ship's Manifest.

108 Ibid.

109 Korman Letter 9.

110 Ibid.

111 *1898 Philadelphia City Directory.*

112 Department of Records, Philadelphia.

113 Ain, "Swislocz—Portrait of a Shtetl."

114 KetubahKetubah.com

115 Alsher, "Observations and English translation of Korman/ Yesersky Letters."

116 Geduld, "From Dowries to Smashed Dishes."

117 Ibid.

118 Ibid.

119 Ibid.

120 Sarah Moss's recollection.

121 I. Barney Moss's recollection.

WORKS CITED

"American Memory." Library of Congress.org. http://www.memory.loc.org.

"Anti-semitism." In *Love To Know Classic Encyclopedia*. http://www.1911encyclopedia.org/Anti-Semitism.

Archangel Michael. "Antiochian Orthodox Christian Archdiocese." http://www.antiochian.org/archangel_michael.

"A Russian Jew's Story." *The New York Times*. August 18, 1890, p. 6. http://query.nytimes.com/mem/archive-free/pdf?res=9401E5DE1239E033A2575BC1A96E9C94619ED7CF

"Brest Fortress." http://www.belarusguide.com/cities/castles/Brest_Fortress.html.

"City Hall." City of Philadelphia, Department of Public Property. http://www.phila.gov/property.

"Emigration 1881–1914: The Plight of Russian Jews." In *Port of Dreams-Emigrant World Ballin Stadt*. http://www.ballinstadt.de.

"Grand Duchy of Lithuania Research Project." JewishFamilyHistory.org. http://www.jewishfamilyhistory.org/grand_duchy_of_lithuania.htm.

"Historic Street Names." City of Philadelphia Department of Records. http://www.phillyhistory.org.

"Lit Brothers." Wikipedia. http://en.wikipedia.org/wiki/Lit_Brothers.

"Modern History, Overview: The Story: 1700–1914." http://www.myjewishlearning.com/history_community/Modern/Overview1700.htm

"N. Snellenburg and Co." Wikipedia. http://en.wikipedia.org/wiki/Snellenburg's#Flagship_Store_and_Factory.

"Obituary, Tony Cliff (Ygael Gluckstein) 1917–2000." Shaw, Martin. http://www.martinshaw.org/cliff.htm.

"Philadelphia City Hall." Wikipedia. http://en.wikipedia.org/wiki/Philadelphia_City_Hall

"Russo-Japanese War." *The Columbia Electronic Encyclopedia*. © 1994, 2000-2006, on Infoplease.© 2000–2007 Pearson Education, publishing as Infoplease.<http://www.infoplease.com/ce6/history/A0842745.html>.

"SEPTA: Philadelphia's Early Transit Services." Southeastern Pennsylvania Transportation Authority. http://www.septa.com.

"Wanamaker's." Wikipedia. http://en.wikipedia.org/wiki/John_Wanamaker_Store Beginnings.

"Women in Steerage Grossly Ill Used." *The New York Times*. December 14, 1909, p. 3. http://www.gjenvick.com/Steerage/1909-WomenInSteerage-ConditionsCalledAppalling.html.

"Yenta." In *The American Heritage Dictionary of the English Language*, Fourth Edition, New York: Houghton Mifflin Company, 2000.

Ain, Abraham. "Swislocz—Portrait of a Shtetl." translated by Shlomo Noble. In *YIVO Bleter* 24 and 25. http://www.shtetlinks.jewishgen.org/Svisloch/abrahamain.htm.

Alsher, Mark. *Observations and English Translation of the Korman/Yesersky Letters and Tenaim*. Philadelphia: 2003.

Antin, Mary. *The Promised Land*. Boston and New York: Houghton Mifflin Company, 1912

Aronson, I. Michael. " The Attitudes of Russian Officials in the 1880s Toward Jewish Assimilation and Emigration." *Slavic Review*, Vol. 34, No. 1 (Mar., 1975). : The American Association for the Advancement of Slavic Studies. http://www.jstor.org/stable/2495871

"Anti-Semitism." In *Encyclopedia Britannica*, Eleventh Edition. Cambridge, 1910.

Atlas of the 23rd, 35th & 41st Wards of the City of Philadelphia. Philadelphia: J. L. Smith, 1910.

Boonin, Harry. "The Jewish Quarter of Philadelphia." http://www.phillyhistory.org/blog/archve/2008/03/05/the-jewish-quarter-of-philadelphia.

Boorstin, Daniel J. *The Americans: The Democratic Experience*. New York: Random House, 1973.

"Brest-Litovsk." In *Encyclopaedia Britannica*, Eleventh Edition. Cambridge,1910

Bromley, George W, and Walter S. Bromley. *Atlas of the City of Philadelphia*. 35th Ward. Philadelphia: G.W.Bromley and Co., 1921.

Cliff, Tony. "1905." *Socialist Worker Review*, January 1, 1985. http://www.marx.org/archive/cliff/works/1985/01/1905.htm

Deganith, Leah. "Rabbi Benjamin Korman." Brisk de-Lita: *Encyclopedia Shel Galuyot Brest Lit(owsk)* Volume II (The Encyclopedia of the Jewish Diaspora,) Editors: E. Steinman, Jerusalem, 1958, translated by Dr. Samuel Chani and Jenni Buch. http://jewishgen.org.

Diehl, Lorraine B., and Marianne Hardart. *The Automat*. Clarkson Potter: New York, 2002.

Feldblyum, Boris. *Russian-Jewish Given Names*. Avotaynu, Inc.: Teaneck, New Jersey, 1998.

Feldman, Kathryn Levy. "The History of the Philadelphia Jewish Federation," 2008. Jewish Virtual Library. http://www.jewishvirtuallibrary.org/jsource/US-Israel/phillyfed.html.

Geduld, Herb. "From Dowries to Smashed Dishes, Marriage Gets Simpler." *Cleveland Jewish News:* January 24, 1997.

Gilbert, Martin. *Atlas of Jewish History*. Weinfeld & Nicolson: London, 1969

Glassman, Deborah G. "Stagecoaches and the Mail in the Geography of Lyakhovichi." 2004. Shtetl links: Lyakhovichi.http://www.shtetlinks.jewishgen.org/lyakhovichi/Stagecoach.htm.

Handler, Davida, Noyek Vitalija Gircyte, Carol Coplin Baker, Alexander Karnovsky, and Judith Langer Caplan. "Revision Lists." Litvak SIG Jewish Gen.org. http://www.jewishgen.org.

Herzen, Alexander. *My Past and Thoughts*. Translated by Constance Garnett., Dwight Macdonald, editor. Berkeley: University of California Press, 1982.

Hickey, Michael. "Demographic Aspects of the Jewish Population in Smolensk Province, 1870s–1914," *Acta Slavica Iaponica*, issue: 19 / 2002, 84–116. Central & Eastern European Online Library. http://www.ceeol.com.

Hickey, Michael C. "People With Pure Souls: Youth Radicalism in Smolensk, 1900–14." In *Revolutionary Russia*, Vol. 20, Issue I, June, 2007.

Howe, Irving. *World of Our Fathers*. New York: Harcourt Brace, 1976, (Book-of-the-Month Club Edition, 1993).

"If I were a Rich Man," from *Fiddler on the Roof*. Jerry Bock: music. Sheldon Harnick: lyrics. Sunbeam Music Inc., 1964.

Jacobs, Joseph and J. de Haas. "The Jewish Colonial Trust (Judische Colonialbank)." http://www.jewishencyclopedia.com/view.jsp?letter=J&artid=270.

"Jewish Colonial Trust Ltd." http://www.jct.co.il/english.html.

Kaplan, M. "The Jews of Brest in the 19th Century." In *Brisk de-Lita: Encyclopedia Shel Galuyot Brest Lit(owsk)* Volume II, *The Encyclopedia of the Jewish Diaspora*, Editors: E. Steinman, Jerusalem: 1958, translated by Dr. Samuel Chani and Jenni Buch. http://www.jewishgen.org.

King, Moses. Philadelphia and Notable Philadelphians. New York: M. King, 1902.

Klier, John D., and Shlomo Lambroza, eds. *Pogroms: Anti-Jewish Violence in Modern Russian History*. Cambridge: Cambridge University, 1992.

Kriwaczek, Paul. *Yiddish Civilization, The Rise and Fall of a Forgotten Nation*, London: Weidenfeld & Nicolson, 2005.

Levy, Bert. "How Passover Will be Observed on the East Side." In *The New York Times*. April 16, 1905.

Levykin, Alexei. "Face to Face With the Czars." *St. Petersburg Times* (Florida). http://www2.sptimes.com/Treasures/TC.2.3.html

Lilly, David P., "The Russian Famine of 1891–92." Chicago: *The College of Humanities and Natural Sciences*, Loyola University, 1994–95. http://www.loyno.edu/~history/journal/1994-5/Lilly.htm

Mann, Stanley. "It Had Its History." In *Hagshama*, World Zionist Organization. http://www.wzo.org.il/en/resources/view.asp?id=1547.

Medvedevsky, Oleg. "Brest, Belarus: Streets and Squares." http://www.city-walk.brest-belarus.org/index.htm.

Miller, Frederic M., " Philadelphia: Immigrant City." Balch Online Resources. http://www.balchinstitute.org/resources/phila_ellis_island.html

Philadelphia City Directory. Philadelphia: James Gospill's Sons. 1907. 1908. 1910.

Roden, Claudia. *The Book of Jewish Food*. New York: Alfred A. Knopf, Inc., 1996

Rosenbaum Bank Passage Order Book Records Database. Compiled by The Philadelphia Jewish Archives Center and the Jewish Genealogical Society of Greater Philadelphia. http://http://www.jewishgen.org.

"Samovars." In *Russian Gifts for the Home*. http://www.russian-gifts-home.com.

Sears, Roebuck & Co. 1908 Catalogue No. 117, replica edition edited by Joseph J. Schroder, Jr., © The Gun Digest Company, Chicago: Follett Publishing Company, 1969.

Shandler, Jeffrey. "Reading Sholem Aleichem from Left to Right." *All About Jewish Theatre*. http://www.jewish-theatre.com/visitor/article_display.aspx?articleid=2039.
Southeastern Pennsylvania Transportation Authority. http://septa.org.

Spiro, Ken. "Crash Course in Jewish History, part 56: The Pale of Settlement." Aish Ha Torah. http://aish.com/literacy/jewishhistory.

Spiro, Ken. "Crash Course in Jewish History, part 57: The Czars and the Jews." Aish Ha Torah. http://aish.com/literacy/jewishhistory.

The Columbia Encyclopedia, sixth edition, New York, Columbia University Press, 2000.

Wainwright, Nicholas, Russell Weigley, and Edwin Wolf. *Philadelphia: A 300-Year History*. New York: W.W. Norton & Company, 1982.

Wawro, Geoffrey. *Warfare and Society in Europe 1792-1914*. Taylor and Francis, London, 2000.

Weisser, Michael R. *A Brotherhood of Memory: Jewish Landsmanshaften in the New World*. Ithaca: Cornell University Press, 1989.

White, Kevin M., "Cardiovascular and Tuberculosis Mortality: The Contrasting Effects of Changes in Two Causes of Death," *Population and Development Review,* Volume 25, Number 2. 1999 http://dx.doi.org/10.1111/j.1728-4457.1999.00289.x

APPENDIX A

How Passover Will Be Observed on the East Side
Written and Illustrated by Bert Levy
The New York Times, *April 16, 1905*

**The Beautiful Sentiment of Opening the Door to the Poor
with Which This Time-Honored Jewish
Festival is Initiated at the Seder Table**

Prosaic miles of streets stretch all around,
Astir with restless, hurried life, and spanned
By arches that with thund'rous trains resound,
And throbbing wires that galvanize the land;
Gin palaces in tawdry splendour stand;
The newsboys shriek of mangled bodies found;
The last burlesque is playing in the town–
In modern prose all poetry seems drowned.
Yet in ten thousand homes this April night,
An ancient people celebrates its birth
To freedom, with a reverential mirth,
With customs quaint and many a hoary rite,
Waiting until, its tarnished glories bright,
Its God shall be the God of all the earth.

Above: Enlarged sections of Bert Levy's
original illustration, shown on page 31.

Next Wednesday evening, the first night of Passover, thousands of the Children of Israel on the great east side will sit by their firesides in faith, hope, and contentment. From the dim haze of antiquity hunted from shore to shore, they have at last found peace—in this country of glorious freedom, where they can at least worship their God in peace, and where their Passover comes without menace of riot and bloodshed.

Sitting among the old men of the Jewish quarter during the coming week, it will require no great stretch of imagination to substitute a Biblical setting of bygone ages for the musty walls of the prosaic east side tenement. As one wanders among the gentle, fervent, and holy worshippers during the Passover week and listens to the soft, low Hebrew melodies, with the strange jingle of rhyme, and watches the quaint ceremonials, the dingy interior of the Shools (synagogues) fade from sight, and in their place the student of biblical lore will see, as it were— in the mind's eye—pictures not of this age.

Imprisoned in an area of narrow, sombre streets, dreary houses darkened by elevated roads and surrounded by sordid sights, the spirit of the Jew that has made him rise superior to thousands of years of persecution comes to his rescue, and on this night of nights—Seder night—he is once again the happy chosen child of the Almighty, for is not Pharoah and all his hosts, with his purple and fine linen, his great treasure cities, at the bottom of the red Sea—smitten—so tradition has it—with 250 plagues?

***

On the first night of Passover, the Jew, in a spirit of charity, will open the door of his house to his poorer brother and invites him to his table, for, on this night of nights, the poor sit with the rich on equal terms.

The beautiful sentiment of opening the door to the poorer brethren has come down from those barbarous times when the Jew on the first night of Passover chanted his prayers behind tightly barred doors, for it was on this night riotous mobs went forth to heap insult and death upon the poor Israelites at their devotions. The roughs were maddened (as they are today in some anti-Semitic countries) and stimulated to all sorts of brutality inflicted upon the harmless members of a noble race by the basely concocted rumor that the blood of Christian children was being used in their ceremonials. The more courageous of the Israelites threw open their doors, and facing the howling mobs, demanded that the leaders should come in and be present at the ceremony to refute the lying stories of the child killing. Hence the ceremony of opening the door, which has in this country become a sentiment instead of a necessity.

In this great republic—the Jews' paradise—the fear of mobs or interference of any sort is indeed remote—woe betide a New York rough who dare emulate the practices toward the Jew of his kind in countries less free and humane than this. To the good Jew the Seder night–the beginning of the week of things unleavened–is a night of extreme happiness. The gathering of the family, the strange symbolic dishes, the bitter herbs, apples, spices, and wines, the roasted bone and lamb, the salted water, and the cups of raisin wine and the lighted candles all placed upon the snow-white table cloth are to him fraught with a meaning sincere and holy.

Few things taste sweeter to him than the matzos (Passover cake) dipped in the raisin wine. The varying species of food at this festive season bring to the elders pleasure in the memory that they are no longer slaves in Egypt and to the younger members a feeling of pride in being free and happy members of the ancient race in a country where there is no persecution and where there are no class distinctions.

The non-Jewish New Yorker looking in upon an east side Jewish family next Wednesday night would marvel at the quaint Old-World atmosphere but a few blocks from busy, prosaic Broadway. The teeming population will have done on this day with the sordid struggle of trade and pour to the Shools (synagogues) and Chevras (small congregations) to lift up its voice in weird, undulating prayers and assonances that have been handed down from the immemorial past.

At the Seder table the youngest male member of the family will ask the father: "Why does this night differ from all other nights?" and the father will reply: "Slaves we have been in Egypt," and he will recite at great length from the Prayer Book the tale of the deliverance from bondage—the most ancient tale in the rituals of the civilized universe, the company meanwhile punctuating the mention of each plague told in the recital by dipping the finger in the glass of raisin wine and jerking it over the shoulder.

***

Throughout the world on this day sons of Judaism will proclaim the belief for which its generations have lived and died. The Jew of Russia will send forth in melancholy cadences the cry of gratitude even from amid his persecution and suffering—in the great cities of Europe, in the diamond fields of South Africa, and in the great cities of the Australian Commonwealth, the declaration will be the same: "Hear, O Israel, the Lord our God is one." The faith that has traveled by the great highroads and queer byways of history to the present generation has bridged the gulf created by separate languages, and Israel is as one in its faith.

On Wednesday, prior to the ushering in of the great festival, the east side streets will provide a wealth of copy for the student of human nature. The vast crowd engaged in buying food for the Passover feasts, the animated traders, peddlers, and pushcart men vying with each other to sell out before the call to worship is sounded, present a scene never to be forgotten. For days the Jewish housewife has been scouring and cleaning the home and searching for the last crumb of leavened bread. On the eve of the first day of Passover the pots and pans, spoons, knives and forks, &c., used throughout the year will be put aside and the special Passover utensils—which have been packed away or bought afresh–will be bought forth. The great round unleavened cakes with their mottled surfaces (called matzos) will take the place of the daily bread and serve to remind the Jew of the days when his forefathers in fleeing Egypt baked bread upon their backs.

APPENDIX B
The Stagecoaches and Mail

This is an excerpt from "Stagecoaches and the Mail in the Geography of Lyakhovichi" by Deborah G. Glassman, copyright 2004, http://www.shtetlinks.jewishgen.org/lyakhovichi/lyakhovichi.html.

A Russian diligence moving along a arrow road. Other travelers were forced to pull off the road to make way for the stagecoach.

Say "stagecoach" to most twenty-first century people and the image that comes immediately to mind is the Western "shoot em up" film. Then, because American history is so abbreviated, Americans tend to think that whatever transportation that was in existence a hundred and fifty years ago, is antique in nature, stretching back into the mists of time. The fact is that the closed passenger wagon drawn by multiple horses is an innovation of the late eighteenth century. It had a heyday of around eighty years. Its start was the development of good postal roads and of governments willing to pay for conveyance of the post. Its end was foreshadowed by the development of a road that could take thousands of pounds of load as well as the mails—the railway. But even after the railroads entered our part of the then Russian Empire in the 1870s, the stagecoaches held on. Conveyances that could go where the railroad lines did not were of great value for several more decades.

The European stagecoach in this time period had a number of forms; the most popular was called a Diligence. In this part of the Russian Empire, the primary horses were those which are today called the Byelorussian Harness Horse which were being crossed regularly with the Ardennes draft horse which were the most popular heavy hauling horse in Russia in the nineteenth century. The larger draft horses were popular everywhere in Europe for the coach trade; they needed to be able to pull loads at 7 to 10 miles per hour for several hours and then do it again the next day. In the US and in western Europe, four to six horses were switched off with others on a journey that might continue twelve to eighteen hours a day and the people would travel around 40 miles a day in the summer and half that in the winter. The coach, those which four horses pulled, would carry eight to twelve passengers, plus baggage, mail, and the driver. Sometimes the driver's seat was counted among the accommodations and then the coach would carry fourteen. Coaches pulled by smaller teams, carried around six people inside. Competition encouraged lines to offer the latest improvements like strap braces that would suspend the coach and make for a ride less subject to jolting. The fare was by the distance traveled.

The Drivers

The small-scale-carrier coachmen of Eastern Europe approached the matter in a different fashion. Keeping four to six horse teams in Europe required either the resources of a government which could leave the teams in authorized way stations while replacements were substituted, or a confidence in law enforcement little in evidence in the region. Small carriers chose the larger horses of Western Europe but tended to operate with only a pair. They were aided by the more level terrain of the region—steeper inclines necessitated more animals to pull heavy loads. They also scheduled routes that would allow them to travel for around six hours and then after a break continue for another few hours. That would be followed by a stop for the night and they would start again with the same horses the next day. It would be an unusual small businessman in Eastern Europe who would have left a healthy horse in the care of a non-relative. The American horse was a little smaller because it was being asked to share work among four horses but a big horse that could do the job as one of two, could reduce the costs of acquisition and maintenance. You could create a business opportunity with fairly low entry barriers, so it was a field that Jews entered in large numbers.

Jews competed as drivers in this field on an equal footing. In some communities Jewish coachmen formed trade associations with other drivers. In some they had sufficient numbers to have their own *schul*. When much, much later, the government of Poland in the 1920s wanted to enforce segregation, they authorized separate seating in schools and separate loading areas for Jewish cabbies in the same legislation. But the common experience of the nineteenth century was not to be abusive or cavalier of the feelings of Jewish drivers. All Jewish teamsters were considered a group essential to the self-defense of Jewish communities—they were accustomed to travelling armed and ready to defend themselves and their freight or passengers from highwaymen or bandits. Many towns have reports of disturbances between Jewish and non-Jewish drivers at inns and supply stations, and both sides appear to have been ready to do physical damage to the other. It is probably a part of the reason that so many of the Belarus (though then Polish) town fire brigades included Jewish teamsters and cab drivers —they were used to working with the horses, racing to a scene, and were seen as tough enough for the job. The network of inns, supply stations, and post offices, also required the skills of blacksmiths, farriers, harness makers, wheelwrights, and other artisans. Because for so long, the Polish nobles, and the subsequent Russian government, profited from keeping their workers on farms uneducated in trade and craft, it was frequently Jews who sought these skills. So just as the inns themselves were largely operated (on lease) by Jews, the skilled crafts related to keeping the nineteenth century passenger coach industry "on the road" were largely performed by Jews. Jews, who wanted to use any of these skills as their passage out of the Russian Pale, found that they now had skills that could get them employed among the household servants of a Jewish First Guild merchant entitled to live outside the Pale. Jewish merchants were not allowed by law to hire Christians, so if he wanted transportation he needed a Jewish driver. Some of the first Jews into St Petersburg, Moscow, Riga, or Warsaw, got there as drivers employed in the households of other Jews. Hoteliers and big-city carriage houses then had a trained group of drivers to draw from and largely employed Jewish drivers for their guests.

Records of the different governors' offices also show them giving short passes to Jewish drivers on essential business. Later this was formalized and Jewish coachmen and freight haulers were allowed to leave the Pale with freight or passengers for two weeks. Looking at the legislation, special permitting, and other documentation, it becomes clear that a critical infrastructure component—transport of people and freight—had been left largely in the hands of a group that was not considered desirable by the Russian government. The only significant item of transportation that they managed to wrest from this group was the mails. And the Jews played a small but significant role in that traffic as well.

The Hope

There in the forest between the rows of trees
Will rest the juniper in the darkness of its sleep,
Its leaves evading, its branches torn away
All vigor, all abundance have passed from its heart.

The storm will rage, the storm will overrun
It will raise the cypress and cedars to sound,
To sway and cheer and even to scream
The ground they will hit becoming stumps.
However, the juniper stands there haughtily
The lashing wind will not its head turn,
The horror and the wailing of the storm
Will not any of its branches or its leaves displace.

The tree will sleep and dream yet many years
That its tree-top will renew to be as once.
Between the majestic noise of the thunder in its power
The voice of the juniper in silence will weep.

The disappointed hope, the eternal hope,
Go from me disappointment – leave me.
Leave me to the depths of my grave
With a blessing of strength, vigor and dew G-d Almighty will anoint me.

The storm will rage, the storm will overrun,
It will raise the cypress and cedars to sound …
In between the noises of the thunder, of the storm,
The voice of the juniper will not be heard …

A.S. Yezersky. Svitslatch, Shvat (January–February) 1898
Translated from Hebrew by Rina Kafri

Samuel Yesersky, photographed at Snellenberg's, Philadelphia.

Avroham Shmuel Yesersky was Yetta's older brother Samuel. His daughter Fannye says that in Russia he was studying to become a rabbi. He wrote this poem in Svisloch shortly before his 18th birthday.

In Philadelphia he became a farmer and later a builder. Samuel wanted to change his name to Isard, as all of his siblings did, but his father, Solomon Yesersky, felt that his eldest son should keep the family name.

A section of the S.S.Breslau manifest. Solomon Yesersky and family are named, starting on line 1.

APPENDIX C

Immigration Information

Passenger	Ship	Departure		Arrival	
		Port	Date	Port	Date
Harris Brody					1882
Rose Brody	Haverford	Liverpool	May 21, 1902	Philadelphia	June 2, 1902
Samuel Yesersky		Liverpool		Philadelphia	1902
Bessie Prilucker	Rhynland	Liverpool	September, 17 1902	Philadelphia	September 30, 1902
Louis Isard	Noordland	Liverpool	September 9, 1903	Philadelphia	September 21, 1903
Hyman Korman	Zeeland	Antwerp	December 3, 1904	New York	December 14, 1904
Yetta Korman	Grosser Kurfurst	Bremen	July 8, 1905	New York	July 18, 1905
Lazar Isard	Patricia	Hamburg	February 23, 1906	New York	March 12, 1906
Solomon Yesersky	Breslau	Bremen	March 25, 1907	New York	April 7, 1907
Miriam Yesersky	"	"	"	"	"
Bella Isard	"	"	"	"	"
Isaac Isard	"	"	"	"	"
Celia Isard	"	"	"	"	"
William Isard	"	"	"	"	"
Oscar Korman	Haverford	Liverpool	November 19, 1913	Philadelphia	December 3, 1913
Hudel Korinman	Stockholm	Gothenburg	May 12, 1921	New York	May 24, 1921
Ida Korman	"	"	"	"	"
Max Korman	"	"	"	"	"
Isidore Korman	"	"	"	"	"
Samuel Korman	"	"	"	"	"
Anna Korman	"	"	"	"	"

APPENDIX D

Names of people in the 36 Letters

This list was a challenge. Almost everyone seems to have multiple names in multiple languages. I have taken the names in the family letters and combined them with the names the people chose when they emigrated to America. They had names in Russian, Yiddish, Hebrew, and English, as well as nicknames and family names.

Family in Brest

Chaim Korman/ Hyman Korman/ Pop

Chaya Ronis Korenman/ Ida Korman (Oscar's wife)

Chaya's new baby/ Anna (Korenman) Korman Bernstein

Chaya's second baby/ Shmuel/ Samuel (Korenman) Korman

Ershl Sidelnik/ Hersch Sidelnik/ Tsvi (Chaim's cousin who accompanied Yente to New York)

Hudel Marzovitz Korinman/ Odel Korman

Leah Merke (Benjamin's sister)

Rabbi Binyomin Korinman/ Benjamin Korman

Tsipe Tsiril - Chaim's cousin

Velvyl Korman/ Wolf Korman (Benjamin's brother)

Yechezkel Korenman/ Oscar Korman

Yoyl Korman (Benjamin's brother)

Friends in Brest

Binyomin the carpenter

David Bialkin

Ershl Pavin

Leah Merke

Noach Brubin- Yaakov's son who fled from the army and went to NY

Peskin

Yaakov Brubin

Yankev Pitikovsky

Yidl Zigman

Yoelik

In Svisloch

Aunt Chaya

Avrohom and Teybe Tsitrovsky - Chaim's friends

Bashke/ Basche Yesersky

Eisen/ Eisik/ Isaac Yesersky Isard

Eliezer Yesersky/ L. Yesersky/Lazar Isard

Freyde

Gitele Slutsky - Yente's friend

Leybe/ Louis Isard

Levintsig

Menachem Rubin and Beylke Liben - engaged to be married

Miriam Brody Yesersky/ Mary Yesersky

Peysekh Altoske

Shlomo Yesersky, Mesersky / Solomon Yesersky

Tsirile/ Zirlo/ Celia Yesersky/ Celia or Sylvia Isard Covelman

Velvele Yesersky/ Willie Yesersky/ William Isard

Yaakov Brody - signed the marriage contract

Yente Yesersky/ Jezierska/Yetta Korman

In New York

Chaim Hersh

Chaim Tsvi Fine

Chaim Tsvi Kidelnik

Kaddish Passman

Rabbi Shimon Passman (friend and relative)

Rabbi Tsvi Passman (friend and relative)

Rabbi Tsvi Sidelik (friend and relative)

Shimon Fine

Yosef Passman/ Joe Passman (Shimon's son, Chaim's cousin)

In Philadelphia

Avrohom Schmuel/ Samuel Yesersky

Blume/ Bessie Priluker Yesersky

Harris Brody

Rokhl Yesersky/ Rose Brody/ Mrs. Broida/ Rosa

Ziske Weinstein

In Zhmerinka, Ukraine

Aunt Pesil Goldfarb

Leyzer Goldfarb - Benjamin's brother-in-law

ACKNOWLEDGEMENTS

I would like to express my thanks to all who helped me write this book. There are so many people who helped me in so many ways.

Elyce Teitelman connected us with Mark Alsher. I had already decided to print and distribute his translations to my family when Sue Popkin and Mickey Langsfeld suggested that the original letters should be properly archived. Sue also suggested that some history would illuminate the letters, and I started to write.

One of the great pleasures of this project has been connecting with my family, as well as those cousins "new, distant, and almost." They have been consistently charming and generous with stories and photographs. They have helped me to know our family in ways I could not have imagined. Again, I kvell.

Angela Fritz, Charlene, Bill, and Blake Richards, and Diane Casey have been my "rocks," always ready for the next version and enthusiastic about my progress. Andrea Gibson, Peter Isard, and Sharon Sumner have read and re-read and made invaluable suggestions. Judy Langsfeld hosted "family fests" and joined me to meet and schmooze and gather stories; Goldie Seiderman joined me at the library and cheered me on. Judy and Richard Gorman encouraged me to publish and Aimee Delman shared publishing experience with me. Janet Tonello understood my design and with her fine eye, skills, and tenacity, brought it to the finished page. Oleg Medvedevsky, in Brest, shared his knowledge of his home. Carol Borgmann's suggested title, Mom and Pop's 36 Smokin' Hot Love Letters, *is just too much fun to leave unmentioned. Henry Neugass's passion for the history of the vanished shtetls, and his work on the website brest-belarus.org., inspire me and set the bar high. Lynne Honickman embraced me and my book, and, with Dr. D. Walter Cohen, brought* 36 Letters, One Family's Story *to the attention of the Jewish Publication Society.*

And Steve Delman has been there, patient and supportive, through the years of writing, re-writing, and computer glitches. His contribution to this book cannot be overestimated.

I have not named everyone who has made a difference and that, in no way, reflects on my appreciation of their efforts. I thank everyone at JPS. I have come into contact with many helpful librarians and archivists, editors and historians. Thank you one and all.

Adrian Andrusier, permission to reproduce archival postcards from his collection.

Art Resource, "I and the Village." Marc Chagall, 1911. Oil on canvas, 6′3 5/8″ x 59 5/8″. Mrs. Simon Guggenheim Fund. The Museum of Modern Art, New York, NY, U.S.A. Digital Image copyright The Museum of Modern Art/Licensed by SCALA / Art Resource, NY. Copyright 2010, Artists Rights Society New York / ADAGP, Pariscopyright ARS, NY.

Bachrach Photographers, Portrait of Hyman Korman, c. 1962. Copyright Peter Blaikie of Bachrach Photography, Ambler, PA.

Deborah G. Glassman, "Stagecoaches and the Mail in the Geography of Lyakhovichi," copyright 2004. http://www.shtetlinks.jewishgen.org/lyakhovichi/lyakhovichi.html.

Free Library of Philadelphia, Market Street Trolley. Print and Picture Collection (Philadelphiana Collection).

Stuart Jackson Gallery, Toronto, "Tsushima." Kiyochika, 1905.

Leonard Korman, his autobiography.

Oleg Medvedevsky, photographs of modern Brest, archival photographs from his collection, and historical information from his website: http://www.city-walk.brest-belarus.org.

Henry Neugass, his photograph of the Mukhavets River in Brest, Belarus, 2007.

NYC Municipal Archives, Delancey Street 1908, photograph by Eugene de Salignac.

Beverly Pomerantz, her family photographs.

Beth Pulsipher, Beth Pulsipher Photography, photographs of pinback portrait buttons.

Janis Quaile, her family photographs.

Goldie Seiderman, her family photographs.

SEPTA, Southeastern Pennsylvania Transportation Authority, a portion of a 1923 PRT Route map and fare tokens of Philadelphia Rapid Transit, a predecessor company of SEPTA.

Fannye Taylor, Bessie Yesersky's Chicken Soup recipe, and "The Hope," Samuel Yesersky's poem.

YIVO Institute for Jewish Research, New York, NY. "Dos ekonomishe lebn fun Sislevitsh," Abraham Ain, YIVO-bleter 25.3 (May–June 1945), 382–401.

The author has made a good faith effort to locate the copyright holder of the 1969 replica of the 1908 Sears, Roebuck Catalogue, No. 117. Neither Follett Publishing Company nor the copyright holder, The Gun Digest, could provide any assistance. Thus the author publishes an image of a Morris Chair in this book under the assumption that it is orphaned and that no existing parties have a claim to the the work's rights.

The author has also made a good faith effort to locate the copyright holder of Brisk de-Lita: *Encyclopedia Shel Galuyot Brest Lit(owsk)*. An attempt to contact the translator was also unsuccessful. Thus the author publishes the excerpt "Rabbi Benjamin Korman" by Leah Deganith under the assumption that it is orphaned and no parties claim the work's rights.